T0006820

NOT A
HOPELESS
CASE

NOT A HOPELESS CASE

6 VITAL QUESTIONS
FROM YOUNG ADULTS
FOR A CHURCH IN CRISIS

HALEE GRAY SCOTT

ZONDERVAN
REFLECTIVE

ZONDERVAN REFLECTIVE

Not a Hopeless Case
Copyright © 2023 by Halee Gray Scott

Requests for information should be addressed to:
Zondervan, *3900 Sparks Dr. SE, Grand Rapids, Michigan 49546*

Zondervan titles may be purchased in bulk for educational, business, fundraising, or sales promotional use. For information, please email SpecialMarkets@Zondervan.com.

ISBN 978-0-310-10672-2 (softcover)
ISBN 978-0-310-11405-5 (audio)
ISBN 978-0-310-10673-9 (ebook)

Unless otherwise noted, Scripture quotations are taken from the ESV® Bible (The Holy Bible, English Standard Version®). Copyright © 2001 by Crossway, a publishing ministry of Good News Publishers. Used by permission. All rights reserved.

Scripture quotations marked CEV are taken from the Contemporary English Version Copyright © 1991, 1992, 1995 by American Bible Society. Used by permission.

Scripture quotations marked NASB are taken from the (NASB®) New American Standard Bible®. Copyright © 1960, 1971, 1977, 1995, 2020 by The Lockman Foundation. Used by permission. All rights reserved. www.lockman.org.

Scripture quotations marked NIV are taken from the Holy Bible, New International Version®, NIV®. Copyright © 1973, 1978, 1984, 2011 by Biblica, Inc.® Used by permission of Zondervan. All rights reserved worldwide. www.Zondervan.com. The "NIV" and "New International Version" are trademarks registered in the United States Patent and Trademark Office by Biblica, Inc.®

Any internet addresses (websites, blogs, etc.) and telephone numbers in this book are offered as a resource. They are not intended in any way to be or imply an endorsement by Zondervan, nor does Zondervan vouch for the content of these sites and numbers for the life of this book.

All rights reserved. No part of this publication may be reproduced, stored in a retrieval system, or transmitted in any form or by any means—electronic, mechanical, photocopy, recording, or any other—except for brief quotations in printed reviews, without the prior permission of the publisher.

Names and identifying characteristics of some individuals have been changed to preserve their privacy.

Cover design: Brand Navigation
Cover image: Unsplash
Interior design: Sara Colley

Printed in the United States of America

23 24 25 26 27 28 29 30 31 32 /TRM/ 12 11 10 9 8 7 6 5 4 3 2 1

To Paul, my husband, my anchor in the storm:
nothing would have been possible without
your steady, strong presence in my life.

CONTENTS

PREFACE

*I believe in Christianity as I believe that
the sun has risen, not only because I see it
but because by it, I see everything else.*
—C. S. Lewis, *The Weight of Glory*

There was a time when I believed the Great American Idea that
your autobiography is your own personal story. Now, after years of
exposure to a rich variety of people, customs, and traditions, I realize
that our personal stories are inextricably linked to the stories of our
fathers, our mothers, and the people of our cultures. For better or for
worse, much of who we are depends on where we came from.[1]

For more than a hundred years, most of the members of my family were cotton farmers, people of the earth who had left the luxuries
of Western Europe to try their hand in a new land. They had enough
courage to traverse the Atlantic and half of the continental United
States territory in search of a better life. They had enough grit and
determination to prevail through both the Great Depression and the
Dust Bowl of Oklahoma. They were a pragmatic, hardworking lot

---

1. Parts of this introduction are from an article I wrote in 2008. See Halee Gray Scott,
"Jesus and Fried Chicken," WomenLeaders.com, June 6, 2008, www.christianitytoday.com
/women-leaders/2008/june/jesus-and-fried-chicken.html. Quoted with permission.

of people who seemed to give little thought to their relationship with God. Jesus was reserved for Sundays—right along with fried chicken, sweet corn on the cob, and creamy mashed potatoes smothered with thick gravy. Their religion had little to do with daily life on the cotton farm.

For much of my life, I believed my ancestors were pragmatically irreligious, too preoccupied with carving a life from the dry, hard earth of West Texas to be concerned with spiritual matters. But recently, in the summer of 2022, I learned from my grandmother that my ancestors' lack of spiritual practice was not because they didn't want to go to church; there simply was no church to go to in the small pioneer town. Once my great-grandfather had rooted out the stubborn mesquite trees, planted rows of cotton, and built a house, and my great-grandmother had stewarded the fields, raised her chickens, and planted her gardens, they turned their attention to building the First Christian Church in Levelland, Texas. Yet even then, there was no discussion of a personal, life-changing relationship with Jesus.

My family's story is not unique among the families that have populated the southern regions of the United States up until the twenty-first century. For those with Jesus-and-fried-chicken faith, being a Christian meant attending church on Sundays and sometimes praying before meals. Christianity did not involve a transformation or a growing, intimate relationship with God. This is the family and the culture in which I was born and raised, and my spiritual journey is the sun-dappled story of how a very real, omnipresent God broke through those false ideas and brought healing to the damage they had caused.

When I was a young girl, my nanny called me "the Preacher" because I always talked about Jesus and tried to apply Scripture to our circumstances. On the way to my great-grandmother's funeral at four years of age, I sensed the somberness of my family. From the back seat, I said brightly, "This is the day the Lord has made. We should rejoice and be glad in it." I remember Nanny and Papa looking back at me, not quite sure what to make of me. In the bathroom of the elementary school playground, a girl named Tasha whacked me across the face. I do not remember why, but I most likely deserved it. For a moment, I stared at her, debating whether to punch back. Instead, I surprised us both and, turning the other cheek toward her, said, "You hit that cheek; hit this one too!" This left her flummoxed, and she fled in the opposite direction.

The point is this: I loved Jesus. I loved his words, who he was, and how he treated others. I desperately, desperately wanted to be like him. Then I grew older, and cracks appeared in my parents' marriage. After their divorce, the people at our Baptist church no longer spoke to us. At thirteen, I resented this. I resented the treatment we received from people who said they believed in God. I resented the leaders, who did not emulate Christ. Their actions spoke so loud I could not hear a word they said.

And so, effectively banished from the family of faith, I drifted into the darkness, embracing a seething atheism and then the casual indifference of agnosticism. I sought transcendence in the euphoria of marijuana, in the company of friends, in books, in education, in late college nights around a campfire. I found, ultimately, only emptiness, sorrow, and profound darkness. As the poet Francis Thompson describes:

> I fled Him, down the nights and down the days;
> I fled Him, down the arches of the years;
> I fled Him, down the labyrinthine ways
> Of my own mind; and in the mist of tears
> I hid from Him, and under running laughter.[2]

But the Hound of Heaven haunted me, breaking into the black night in which I had cloaked myself. I came to believe the Story was

---

2. Francis Thompson, "The Hound of Heaven" (1893), warwick.ac.uk/fac/arts/english /currentstudents/undergraduate/modules/fulllist/second/en227/texts/thompson-hound.pdf, accessed January 2, 2022.

true and that unbelief demanded more faith than Christianity. The proof was the hollow wreckage of my life. On my twenty-first birthday, at 2:00 a.m. after a long shift waiting tables at Applebee's, as the rain drizzled down the windshield of my Nissan Sentra, I committed my life again to Jesus in the parking lot of my apartment complex.

Not long after, I was raped by the youth pastor at my church, where I had served on the youth team from the moment I rededicated my life to Christ. I have extensively detailed the experience elsewhere and do not wish to revisit the story here.[3] Suffice it to say, broken, abused by a person of the clergy, I was faced with a series of questions: Did I believe God was good, even after all this? Did I even believe in a god at all? And if so, how would I continue to serve him when I could not enter the doors of a church without breaking apart with crippling anxiety? Luckily (blessedly?), I found work at a Christian nonprofit and there found a fellowship of believers who surrounded me and comforted me, even if they did not know why I needed safety and comfort.

During this period, I attended regular meetings with a biblical counselor. Apart from the trauma of the assault, the shame of my life choices choked my soul like purple clementis chokes a trellis. Like Nathaniel Hawthorne's Hester Prynne, I felt as though I carried all my sin on the outside, visible for all to see. The weight of my shame was so great I wanted to give up, give in. As I told the counselor my life story, I cast myself as the villain in every scenario. I wanted her to tell me I was a hopeless case. But she did not. She simply said, "My dear child, God must love you so much."

Her response was so disarming that in time I decided that, despite it all, I did believe God was good. No, I was *convicted* of the fact. I was equally convicted I ought to spend my life ensuring, to the best of my ability, that what happened to me would not happen to others.

---

3. Halee Gray Scott, "#MeToo: I Was Raped by My Pastor," *Washington Post*, October 16, 2017, www.washingtonpost.com/news/acts-of-faith/wp/2017/10/16/metoo -i-was-raped-by -my -pastor/.

I would not let people languish in darkness as I had. I would not let people believe they are hopeless cases. I would not let people be turned away from the faith because of the behavior of Christian leaders. As lofty and out of my control as those goals might have been, they were my only path forward, my only way to go on. And so, thanks to the unwavering support of my husband, Paul, I pursued an MA in religion at Azusa Pacific University and ultimately studied leadership and spiritual formation at Talbot School of Theology.

At twenty-seven, I began teaching undergraduate courses at Azusa Pacific University, always feeling somewhat of an impostor. That feeling was amplified when, at thirty-one and six months pregnant with my daughter Ellie, I taught my first graduate course: Church and Society. Nearly all of my thirty students were older than me. One African American man had ministered in South Central Los Angeles longer than I had been alive. The first night of class, he challenged me on every point. The second night, I shared my testimony, and that man became my biggest ally. That is when I learned there are two types of authority: the authority we receive from positions, training, degrees, or street cred; and the authority we get from lived experience.

When I was growing up, my dad would laugh and say, "Halee, you ask too many questions," and so I parlayed that skill into journalism and eventually sociological research. Though I still teach graduate courses today, research, the asking of questions, is my deepest vocational love. Objectivity is the goal of every researcher worth their salt, and throughout my tenure as a researcher, I have put this goal ever before me. However, I cannot be divided from my story any more than my story can be divided from those who came before me, so this book is written on the foundation of two types of authority: my training as a researcher and my lived experience. For I, too, once was a None, a no-way, a no-how, an absolutely-not. Their questions were once my questions. It was the surprise of my life when, during the course of this research, I discovered I was far from alone.

I understand the questions of young adults. We ignore them not just at our own peril but at the peril of the souls who dwell in the darkness. When we turn deaf ears to the critiques, when we focus on numerical growth rather than spiritual growth, when we become desensitized to the central message and calling of Jesus, when we experience fragmentation in the church over issues of gender, worship, service, and textual interpretation, we risk reducing our faith to a Jesus-and-fried-chicken faith. With Jesus there is no "and." There is only Jesus, the dusty-footed itinerant preacher who ushered in a revolution in the way we understand and relate to God. May we bring the person and character of Christ to bear on the questions of our time.

ACKNOWLEDGMENTS

This book was born of the labor and love of many.

First, I'd like to thank Betsy Nesbit Wagner, my friend, colleague, fellow dreamer, and strategist. You are one of a kind, my friend, and I am so grateful for your support and guidance.

Second, this project would not be possible without the team of researchers who lived into the stories of the churches and young adults: Ryan Beerwinkle, Reid Bervik, Jonathan Carr, Cole Comstock, Vondae Donaldson, Hunter Hambrick, Elizabeth Klemt, Taylor Miskel, Brian Moore, Victoria Mosko, Karla Valencia, and Christopher Wynn. You all are so gifted, so intelligent, and I am so honored to have had the opportunity to work with you and learn from you.

Third, many other people from Denver Seminary provided valuable support throughout the tenure of the project, including Mark Young, Wendi Gowing, Mary Rivera, Merri Haskins, and Pam Dill.

Finally, I would like to thank my family. Dad, thank you for fielding all the many questions I posed when I was young. You gave me the freedom to ask questions and seek answers, and I use those skills today. Eliana and Vivi, my daughters, thank you for your curiosity, your wisdom, and your company. I'm so proud of the young women you are becoming. Paul, as always, thank you for your strong and steady presence in my life.

PART ONE

WHAT, HOW, WHO, WHEN

ONE

THE WHAT

Embracing the Power of a Question

It is easier to judge the mind of a man by
his questions rather than his answers.
—Pierre-Marc-Gaston de Lévis, *Maximes et réflexions*
sur différents sujets de morale et de politique

What is more powerful than a question?

Questions focus the mind. Like the hook of a question mark, they capture the reader's or hearer's attention. Questions hijack our brains so we can focus on nothing else. Try this: What is your favorite season of the year?

Chances are, after reading the question, images of budding green on barren tree branches; memories of long, lazy days at the lake or beach; the year's first blue norther signaling the approach of autumn; or cold evenings spent by the fireplace with snow flurries swirling outside the window came to mind, sweeping away other thoughts. The latest research in neuroscience indicates that, contrary to popular belief, the brain cannot multitask. In his book *Brain Rules*, neuroscientist John Medina explains there are four shifts in the brain that must occur to switch from one task to another.[1] Medina concludes, "The best you can say is that people who appear to be good at multitasking actually have good working memories, capable of paying attention to several inputs *one at a time*."[2] Thus, when you pose a question, you command the hearer's attention.

Questions have crumpled empires. Even as Rome was attacked by outside forces, around AD 476 the aristocracy questioned the empire's oppressive taxation and fled to the countryside to establish independent fiefdoms, lightening Rome's dwindling coffers even further. In the 1450s, the young sultan Mehmed II questioned how to fell Constantinople's Theodosian Walls, the strongest fortifications ever built in the ancient or medieval worlds. At Griffin's Wharf in 1773, American colonists questioned the practice of paying taxes to a government authority without corresponding representation in Parliament that would give them a say in the government's activities. Or in the poetic language of Lin-Manuel Miranda, the colonists asked, "Why should a tiny island across the sea regulate the price of tea?"[3] Across the Atlantic, a growing gloom gathered around the French peasantry in the 1780s, their hunger and strife stoking

---

1. John Medina, *Brain Rules: Twelve Principles for Surviving and Thriving at Work, Home, and School* (Seattle: Pear Press, 2014), 116–17. These four shifts are (1) the Shift Alert, when the blood rushes to your anterior prefrontal cortext, alerting a shift in attention, (2) Rule Activation for Task 1, the first of a two-part message that "is a search query to find the neurons" that can complete the new task, (3) Disengagement, when distractions cause the brain to disengage from the activity, and (4) Rule Activation for Task 2, returning to the original task.

2. Ibid., 117.

3. "Farmer Refuted," *Hamilton*, music and lyrics by Lin-Manuel Miranda, directed by Thomas Kail (New York: Richard Rodgers Theatre, June 2016), aired July 3, 2020, on Disney+.

their questions about vast economic inequality, unfair taxation, and tithing.

Questions lead to innovation. Most inventions begin with questions. Early humans questioned how to more easily impact the natural environment by cutting through branches, tree bark, and digging, thus leading to the invention of the hand ax. Later, they questioned how to control fire in order to stay warm, provide light at night, ward off predators, and cook food. Sir Isaac Newton kept hundreds of notebooks (then known as his "waste books") detailing questions that led to the foundations of modern calculus and an understanding of the motion of comets. Legend says that when Newton's cats were constantly interrupting his experiments, he invented a cat door, instructing a Cambridge carpenter to cut a small hole at the bottom of his door so the cats could roam freely without disturbing him.

Throughout the nineteeth century, inventors questioned the safety and efficacy of open flames and gas lighting and began work on prototypes of the electric light bulb, which Thomas Edison perfected.

Steve Jobs questioned how to combine a celluar phone and the iPod, leading to the invention of the iPhone.

When addressing a need through invention, one cannot underestimate the importance of questions or scientific inquiry. Dr. Shirley Ann Jackson, the first black woman to earn a PhD from MIT and one of the contributors to the invention of telecommunications, argues the need for scientific inquiry: "We need to go back to the discovery, to posing a question, to having a hypothesis."[4]

Questions are central to the pedagogy of the greatest teachers. Socrates believed in the disciplined practice of asking thoughtful questions to stoke critical thinking in his students. The Socratic method

---

4. *Charlie Rose*, "Science Series: The Promise of Science," hosted by Charlie Rose and Paul Nurse, featuring Harold Varmus, Shirley Ann Jackson, Bruce Alberts, and Lisa Randall, aired April 7, 2008, on PBS, 11:58, charlierose.com/videos/14644.

is still used today, especially in medical and legal education. In the sixteenth century, scholars in countries such as France, Germany, and Switzerland referenced the Socratic method in their work. English hymn writer Isaac Watts wrote in his book *The Improvement of the Mind* that the Socratic method "represents the form of a dialogue or common conversation, which is a much more easy, more pleasant, and a more sprightly way of instruction, and more fit to excite the attention and sharpen the penetration of the learner, than solitary reading or silent attention to a lecture."[5] Published in the mid-eighteenth century, this was the first print reference to the Socratic method in the American colonies.

The Oxford Socratic Club was a student club dedicated to providing "an open forum for the discussion of the intellectual difficulties connected with religion in general and with Christianity in particular."[6] According to Stella Aldwinckle of the Oxford Pastorate, the most obvious choice for president of the club was C. S. Lewis, who enthusiastically served as president from 1942 until 1954. The club met on Monday evenings, with agnostics and atheists bringing their questions about religion. Lewis believed the club offered the opportunity to air sincere questions and allowed opposite sides to express their position, guarding against rumor, dogmatism, and group hostilities.[7]

Questions play a crucial role in the Old Testament. God has always welcomed and engaged doubters. Throughout the Old Testament, we see God engage with the questions his creation put before him as long

---

5. Isaac Watts, *The Improvement of the Mind* (Baltimore: Bayly and Burns, 1838), 105, www.google.com/books/edition/The_Improvement_of_the_Mind/TAmod VNefeoC?hl= en &gbpv=1.

6. Stella Aldwinckle, quoted in Phyllis Levers, "The Christian, the Skeptic, and the Club," letter to the editor, *Christian Science Monitor*, August 10, 1994, www.csmonitor.com /1994/0810/letter1.html, accessed September 16, 2022.

7. Christopher Mitchell, "University Battles—C. S. Lewis and the Oxford University Socratic Club," C. S. Lewis Institute, January 7, 2010, www.cslewisinstitute.org/resources /university-battles-c-s-lewis-and-the-oxford-university-socratic-club/.

as they did so with the right spirit. When God called Moses out of the desert to free his people from slavery, Moses replied, "Who am I?" (Ex. 3:11). This question is not unlike what many of us feel when God calls us to do something. When God decided to destroy Sodom, Abraham asked, "Will you indeed sweep away the righteous with the wicked?" (Gen. 18:23). David, whom God declared was "a man after his own heart" (1 Sam. 13:14), penned fifty-one questions to God, mostly concerning the nature of God's justice. The prophet Habakkuk longed to know when God would intervene in the violence he saw before him (Hab. 1:2). And of course Job, who lost all that he had, bitterly questioned God and was rebuked, "Who is this that darkens counsel by words without knowledge?" (Job 38:2).

Questions are central to the New Testament as well. According to one author, in the four gospels Jesus asks 307 questions.[8] These questions invite listeners to engage in deep reflection and, ultimately, the possibility of transformation. One of my favorite verses in the New Testament is Jesus' question: "Do you want to get well?" (John 5:6 NIV). This question chases me, haunts me, and causes me to examine my interior life in great detail, like the millimeter wave imaging machines at airport security. Do you, Halee, *want* to be well? As the poet Rainer Maria Rilke instructs, for now, I live with the question, with the hope that one day I might live my way into the answer.

On the other hand, in the four gospels Jesus is asked 183 questions.[9] How many did he directly answer without first asking a counterquestion? Few.[10] When Peter asked, "Lord, how often will my brother sin against me, and I forgive him? As many as seven times?"

8. Martin Copenhaver, *Jesus Is the Question: The 307 Questions Jesus Asked and the 3 He Answered* (Nashville: Abingdon, 2014).

9. Ibid., 16.

10. John Dear, *The Questions of Jesus: Challenging Ourselves to Discover Life's Great Answers* (New York: Doubleday, 2004), xxii; Eric Burtness, *Book of Faith Lenten Journey: Beyond Question* (Minneapolis: Augsburg Fortress, 2012), 9.

Jesus answered, "I do not say to you seven times, but seventy-seven times" (Matt. 18:21–22). To the Pharisee's question about why Moses commanded men to give a certificate of divorce, Jesus answered, "Because of your hardness of heart Moses allowed you to divorce your wives, but from the beginning it was not so" (Matt. 19:8). His other direct answers were:

- "The most important is, 'Hear, O Israel: The Lord our God, the Lord is one. And you shall love the Lord your God with all your heart and with all your soul and with all your mind and with all your strength.' The second is this: 'You shall love your neighbor as yourself,'" which he said when a scribe asked which commandment was most important (Mark 12:28–34).
- "Because of your little faith," which he said when the disciples asked why they were not able to heal a boy's epilepsy (Matt. 17:16–20).
- "Go into the city, and a man carrying a jar of water will meet you. Follow him," which he said when the disciples asked where he wanted to eat the Passover meal (Mark 14:13).
- "It is he to whom I will give this morsel of bread when I have dipped it," which he said when Peter asked who would betray Jesus (John 13:26).
- "I am," which he said when the high priest asked if he was "the Christ, the Son of the Blessed" (Mark 14:61–62).

Apart from these instances, Jesus answered questions with questions of his own, questions that drove the hearer to a deeper source of wisdom and learning. He did this from early childhood. When Jesus stayed behind in Jerusalem while his parents returned to Nazareth, Mary asked, "Son, why have you treated us so? Behold, your father and I have been searching for you in great distress." He answered, "Why were you looking for me? Did you not know that I must be in my Father's house?" (Luke 2:48–49). When Jesus was teaching and preaching the gospel, the chief priests and the scribes along with the elders asked him, "Tell us by what authority you do these things, or who it is that gave you this authority." Jesus answered, "I also will ask you a question. Now tell me, was the baptism of John from heaven or from man?" (Luke 20:2–4).

ASKING QUESTIONS AT CHURCH

From the beginning, when Mary asked Gabriel, "How will this be, since I am a virgin?" (Luke 1:34), questions have swirled like fiery embers around the person of Christ and those who follow him, and every age brings different questions. Because of a confluence of changing cultural conditions brought on by technology, civil unrest, distrust of authority, skepticism of government institutions (and institutions in general), competing metanarratives, and fake news, the questions people are asking today are potent and demand thoughtful engagement. These are questions such as "Why should I sit through a sermon when I can listen to a podcast?" or "Why should I trust my parents, teachers, or pastors to answer tough questions when I can google the answers?" or "Who can I trust to listen to my real concerns if everyone seems to have some kind of agenda?"

Some of the most vigorous questions are posed by the Nones, the heavily researched group comprised of mostly young adults who affiliate with no religion. Amid the national and global crises of the early aughts and 2010s, Pew Research Center identified a sharp rise of the Nones—particularly noted among those aged twenty-three to twenty-nine—and documented this shift in the landmark 2012 study *"Nones" on the Rise.*[11] In just five years, from 2007 to 2012, the number of people who claimed "no affiliation" to any religion rose from

11. Pew Research Center, *"Nones" on the Rise: One-in-Five Adults Have No Religious Affiliation*, October 9, 2012, 10–16, www.pewforum.org/2012/10/09/nones-on-the-rise.

15 percent to 20 percent, meaning one in every five Americans has no religious affiliation.[12]

A 2018 Pew Research Center article notes, "Six-in-ten religiously unaffiliated Americans—adults who describe their religious identity as atheist, agnostic or 'nothing in particular'—say the questioning of religious teachings is a very important reason for their lack of affiliation."[13] Although Peter instructed us to be "prepared to make a defense to anyone who asks you for a reason for the hope that is in you; yet do it with gentleness and respect" (1 Peter 3:15), many of the young adults in the Pew Research Center study did not experience that in their home churches. In a similar study, a five-year project from Barna revealed that one of the six reasons people leave the church is because they find it to be "unfriendly to those who doubt."[14]

Although the Pew Research Center popularized the term *Nones*, sociologists and other scholars have known about this group since the early twentieth century, when they were described as "free-thinker," "non-affiliated," or "Independent Christians."[15] In 1968, sociologist Glenn Vernon of the University of Utah urged religious scholars to accept "None" as a valid category of religious behavior that ought to be further studied. He argued this category was a "religious phenomenon which appears to be of significance and . . . provides a more complete understanding of religious behavior."[16]

---

12. Ibid. 9.

13. "Why America's 'Nones' Don't Identify with a Religion," Pew Research Center, August 8, 2018, www.pewresearch.org/fact-tank/2018/08/08/why-americas-nones-dont-identify-with-a-religion/.

14. The Barna Group, "Six Reasons Young Christians Leave Church," BioLogos, June 5, 2017, biologos.org/articles/six-reasons-young-christians-leave-church. The other five reasons are: (1) the church feels overprotective, making Christianity feel "stifling, fear-based and risk-averse," (2) teens and twentysomethings experience Christianity as shallow, (3) churches come across as antagonistic to science, (4) young Christians' experiences related to church are simplistic and judgmental, and (5) they wrestle with "the exclusive nature of Christianity."

15. Glenn M. Vernon, "The Religious 'Nones': A Neglected Category," *Journal for the Scientific Study of Religion* 7, no. 2 (1968): 220n3, doi.org/10.2307/1384629.

16. Ibid., 220.

Today, current research suggests the following about the Nones:

1. They tend to be younger, with the steepest change in those aged twenty-three to twenty-nine. The 2012 Pew Research Center study attributed the rise primarily to "generational replacement, the gradual supplanting of older generations by newer ones."[17]
2. They are a weather vane pointing to a decline in religious commitment among Americans.
3. They often describe themselves as "spiritual but not religious."[18]
4. They believe the church is too political.
5. They believe the church is too concerned with money and power.
6. They are troubled with abuses of power, church hurt, and church scandals.[19]

The study from Pew Research Center caused a national furor, stoking response in the form of books, articles, editorials, and further studies. It has uniquely affected the work of pastors and Christian leaders, who—despite the abundance of resources available—still struggle to reach this generation. The more apocalyptic studies they hear, the more hopeless they feel about their mission and calling.

So, for all we know about the Nones on paper, I wanted to know their questions and, more important, their stories. Stories provide textured detail that facts and statistics often miss. For example, statistics tell us the questioning of religious teaching contributes to the Nones' lack of affiliation; these facts do not speak to the many Nones who first sought their answers from the church and were shut down or directly ignored. Stories provide the background for why a question is asked in the first place.

---

17. Pew Research Center, *"Nones" on the Rise*, 10.
18. Ibid., 20.
19. Ibid., 10, 23, 29.

GIVING OXYGEN TO QUESTIONS

Questions are like seeds buried in the rich, dark soil of our hearts. Nurtured with oxygen and water, they unfold into that which they were meant to become. Absent these conditions, they wither in the dark. Given oxygen and room to breathe, the next generation can impact the whole world with just a few changes. Maybe we can help them do this by listening more (however hard this is at first) to their stories instead of focusing on principles and statistics. As you will read in the following chapters, the culture in which we live demands rigorous examination by Christians to confidently answer the questions that young adults raise.

Over the years of my journey with the Nones and the pastors who seek to help them, I have learned that those most resistant to Christianity are people whose questions did not receive enough attention when they were asked. These Nones lacked oxygen in their faith communities as children and teenagers. This book is the story of their questions about faith and spirituality—the questions of young adults who are lost and want to be found—and the questions of pastors who seek to find them.

QUESTIONS FOR INDIVIDUAL AND SMALL GROUP REFLECTION

1. Is it easy for you to ask questions? Why or why not?
2. Are there some settings in which it is easier to ask questions than others? If so, which ones and why?
3. Are you encouraged or discouraged to ask questions in your home or faith community?

4. If you are able to freely ask questions in your home or faith community, what does that tell you about the person willing to engage your questions?

5. When you receive answers to your questions, how well do you receive them?

6. If you are not able to freely ask questions in your home or faith community, how does that make you feel about those around you?

7. The answer to almost any question we can ask is at our fingertips through our phones, iPads, and computers. What are some questions you have that Google cannot answer? How important is it to your faith that they be answered?

8. What steps can we take in our faith communities to better understand the questions posed by young adults who are Christians?

9. What steps can we take in our faith communities to better understand the questions posed by young adults who are not Christians?

10. What kind of situation is best for tackling different questions (e.g., during a forum, in a discussion group, over a meal at a church member's home)? Why do you prefer this type of setting?

TWO

THE HOW

Meeting the Nones Face-to-Face

> *The social brain is in its natural habitat when we're*
> *talking with someone face-to-face in real time.*
> —Daniel Goleman, "Focus on How You Connect"

On a warm summer evening in June, I gathered a group of atheists and agnostics to discuss their views on Christianity, to get their perspective on faith and religion and why they have opted to reject religion and, in some cases, even spirituality. Setting sunlight glanced off the green leaves of the towering cottonwood trees that lined the street as I nervously approached a modest Craftsman-style home, arms laden with burritos, salsa, and soft drinks. When I had put out the call for focus group participants on social media and through friends, I was concerned no one would respond. I needed just eight people for a strong focus group, but even that felt ambitious. Why would agnostic and atheistic young adults be interested in discussing a faith they did not have?

I need not have worried: they were eager to discuss their views on Christianity, religion, and spirituality. As I entered the home, I was greeted warmly by three young women who took the catering bags, drinks, and utensils from my arms and started setting out the food. As participants trickled in, they, too, chipped in to set the table for dinner. By the time everyone showed up, there were fifteen people total—more than I expected, and a lot for a focus group, but manageable. I could not help but wonder again: Why had all these people chosen to spend an evening talking to me about a faith they did not proclaim?

We sat in a circle in the living room, and as we dove into our thick Moe's burritos, our chat was light and lively. Still in their mid-to-late twenties, the people in the group had highly successful careers. They were geotechnical engineers, astrophysics engineers, teachers, and journalists. I strove to create a neutral, nonjudgmental environment, and they spoke with me openly and honestly. At one point a young man held up his Bible, thick with Post-it Notes and bookmarkers, and said, "My Bible is thicker than any Christian I know because I read the whole Bible and annotated everything I hate about God." As I was to learn over the course of our conversation, all of them had grown up in religious households, and all of them had walked away from religion. These were Nones, people who affiliate with no religion.

THE WALK THROUGH ATHENS

On his second missionary journey, the apostle Paul's ministry in Berea was cut short when Jewish leaders from Thessalonica arrived and agitated the crowds. Leaving Silas and Timothy, Paul continued to Athens, where he awaited them. Athens, though no longer a city of political import, was still the birthplace of Western philosophy, renowned as the city of Pericles, Socrates, Plato, Sophocles, and Euripides, men whose teachings rivered down through the centuries, shaping intellectual discourse and thought to this day. The city overflowed with idols. The author and natural philosopher Pliny, a contemporary of Paul, recorded that there were more than thirty thousand public idols in the city, not counting the innumerable private ones in Athenian homes. Petronius, a Roman courtier and satirist, cheekily wrote that it was "easier to find a god in Athens than a man."[1]

While Paul waited for Silas and Timothy, he walked through Athens, surveying the idols, the statues to various gods. Acts 17:16 records that he was *paroxyneto*, provoked, sharpened, and exasperated by a city so laden with idols. But walking through Athens gave Paul a glimpse into the Athenian soul, and he found a connection point: the altar inscribed to "the unknown god" (v. 23). Paul's steps led him eventually to the Areopagus, also known as the Hill of Ares or Mars Hill, a prominent rock outcropping that served as a meeting place for Athenians and foreigners to articulate and hear new ideas. Here, Paul delivered one of the most dramatic sermons of his career.

THE SPIRITUALITY OF THE NONES

"The word 'spirituality,'" writes theologian Alister McGrath, "draws on the Hebrew word *ruach*—a rich term usually translated as 'spirit,' yet includes a wide range of meanings including 'spirit' yet extending to 'breath' and wind.'"[2] Thus, McGrath concludes, spirituality is "about the life of faith—what drives it and motivates it, and what people find helpful in sustaining and developing it."[3] In recent times, academics, psychologists, and laypeople alike have sought to determine

---

1. B. F. Cocker, *Christianity and Greek Philosophy* (New York: Carlton and Lanahan, 1870; Project Gutenberg, 2008), 100, www.gutenberg.org/files/27571/27571-h/27571-h.htm.
2. Alister McGrath, *Christian Spirituality: An Introduction* (Malden, MA: Blackwell Publishing, 1999), 1–2.
3. Ibid., 2.

the nature of "secular spirituality." In the book *The Oxford Handbook of Secularism*, Robert C. Fuller notes eight central attributes of secular spirituality: "eclecticism, self-growth, relevance to life, self-direction, openness to wonder, authenticity beyond churches, metaphysical explanations, and communal and ecological morality."[4]

For four months, since beginning my role at Denver Seminary as the Young Adult Initiative director,[5] I, in effect, walked through Athens. I buried myself in research about the Nones. Though studies painted a confident, detailed picture of this group, there seemed to be no end to what we know about them. We know their average age (twenty-three to twenty-nine), their most common race (Caucasian), and the gender most likely to be a None (men). We know that many, but not all, describe themselves as "spiritual, but not religious." We know that some, but not all, even attend religious services.

If not church, I wondered, *then where do the Nones go to find spiritual fulfillment in the Denver metro area?* So I walked through Athens. I went to Denver's most celebrated craft breweries, ordering fancy mocktails and surveying the spaces. *This is where people can gather*, I thought, noting the warmth of the environments, the rooms for board games and large televisions for movies or sports events. At one brewery a female bartender called out peoples' names as they came through the door. Regulars. Young adults.

I rolled out my mat for yoga classes and joined a guided meditation session, perched anxiously beside a statue of Buddha. During my month of CrossFit classes, I learned that at thirty-nine my knees crackled like Rice Krispies (really, already?) and also how very like church CrossFit is: the WOD (workout of the day) is their liturgy; the partner you are paired with is your accountability and source of

---

4. Robert C. Fuller, "Secular Spirituality," in *The Oxford Handbook of Secularism*, ed. Phil Zuckerman and John R. Shook (New York: Oxford University Press, 2017), 571–86.

5. The Young Adult Initiative was launched and funded by Lilly Endowment Inc. to understand how churches can reach young adults—the group most likely to consider themselves as unaffiliated with any religion. See the section "The Kaleo Project" later in this chapter.

encouragement; the teacher is your shepherd and leader to better fitness. I ran marathons, half-marathons, and the famed BOLDERBoulder. I spent the equivalent of weeks on Colorado trails, summiting four-teeners, traversing mountainsides, and climbing the Manitou Incline.

These are not the idols of Athens, but they are the secular spaces people go to today, especially here in Denver, Colorado, to find spiritual meaning and fulfillment without the religious baggage that the Nones often associate with church.

Yet even that was not enough for me to understand the soul of the Nones. For all the things we know about the Nones from data gathering and surveys, for all we know on paper, we know very little about their stories and the questions or criticisms they have about the Christian faith.[6]

It is one thing for a person to mark a survey that will be analyzed later with scores of other surveys by researchers far removed from the life context of survey respondents. It is another thing to sit with these people in a room late into the night, mining for the reasons and experiences that lie beneath what surveys tell us, to witness their anger, to empathize with their tears. One can learn more from a single teardrop than from stacks of books and research reports.

This is why I convened the group of young adult atheists and agnostics. On that night, these young adults were my teachers, and I, their student. This is what I learned.

THE MOST SIGNIFICANT SOURCE OF SPIRITUAL INFLUENCE

Throughout millennia, religion has served as a source of spiritual influence for billions of people around the globe. But where do those

---

6. One notable exception to this is the work of Kenda Creasy Dean, professor of youth, church, and culture at Princeton Theological Seminary in New Jersey. I highly recommend her book *Almost Christian: What the Faith of Our Teenagers Is Telling the American Church.*

who reject religion turn for spiritual influence? For this group of millennials, the overwhelming answer was their parents. "My parents, for sure, [have been the main source of spiritual influence]," said Max,[7] "in terms of modeling good behavior. When you find yourself in situations that are sort of uncomfortable, and you're like, 'What am I going to do?' you kind of naturally fall back on what your mom would do or what your dad would do in that situation. That's what compels me to take certain actions."

Others described their parents as having a negative effect on their spirituality. After Max, Claire piped in, "My mom is very Christian, and I think part of the reason I am not is because she is. So I would say she is a very strong spiritual influence in my life and possibly a religious influence but not in a pushing-me-toward-church kind of way. . . . I very much admire and respect her beliefs, but I don't agree with her."

Leah concurred: "My parents both influenced me in a spiritual way, but like in a negative sense. That deterred me from any real semblance of spirituality or religiosity." She continued, "My dad is very evangelical—super, super religious—whereas my mom is more nebulously spiritual." Leah described her father as hypocritical, a person not living in accordance with his professed beliefs. Because of this, for a long time, she believed all Christians were hypocritical and insincere.

Karen attended a Catholic school for most of her life, and she, too, found Christians hypocritical: "School wasn't . . . um . . . the best, and that's where the hypocrisy became really apparent to me. Because it wasn't just my parents [being hypocritical]; it was all of my teachers, all of my friends, all of their families, all of these people who identified as Catholics. So it's really easy to say there are flaws with [Christianity] because there are hundreds of people you can look at and find things wrong [with the way they act]."

---

7. Unless otherwise noted, names of individuals and churches have been changed.

Unlike the others, Madison credited her spirituality to herself. "I am the person who has the biggest spiritual influence in my life," she said. "I don't really turn to anybody else. I just think, *Okay, what do you think about this, Madison? Do you believe this?*"

I prodded her gently, "How do you figure out what you think? How do you find that direction?"

"Good question," she replied, "I base a lot of things off of feeling. And so, I check in with myself: *Does this make you feel uncomfortable?*"

THE MAIN BARRIERS TO CHRISTIANITY

For some, legalistic parents and home church congregations were the biggest barriers to Christianity. Leah described her life as a PK, a pastor's kid, and how the church had been a second home until she began to ask questions about certain teachings. "When I started to ask harder questions about my faith, people distanced themselves from me. I just realized that things weren't right and . . . nobody actually cared. I was like, 'I thought these people were my friends. I thought these leaders cared about my growth as a person, but [their friendship and care] was nonexistent.'"

"That must have been really painful," I said to her quietly.

"It was," she replied. "I felt really rejected. They can't be friends with me. They can't."

Max chimed in, "So wrong. It's like their love, whatever, is super conditional."

The rest of the group agreed that Christians were not loving to those outside their religion. Kate asked, "So, are there beautiful, loving connections being made outside [Christianity]? Do [Christians] really care? Are [Christians] bridging that gap? With people who are scarred?"

Others said the political inclinations of the church were their biggest barrier. One participant leaned in passionately, "You know the evangelical crowd voted for Trump by like 80 percent—the overwhelming majority—and he says things I would never, ever, ever say to anybody. No matter how angry I was or intoxicated I was, I would never say that stuff."

Jeff agreed: "I think you can clearly say that Trump is, like, guided by the basest of emotions and self-service. I just don't understand how you can conflate . . . how you can believe both in Jesus and also Trump as your president to carry out your ideals in the real world. It just seems like there's a contradiction there."

For these Nones, science was also a significant barrier to Christianity. Crista explained: "I mean, we're just now realizing in the last hundred years how small we are. . . . [The universe] is so much bigger than we ever expected. And also, we're not the center of the universe; we're actually really far off to a side. I mean, we're actually less than a speck of dust. There are more galaxies in the universe than there are grains of sand on the earth. And we are on one planet around one of those stars, and to think we would be so solipsistic to believe that all of this was made for us is the fundamental reason I just don't get it."

Legalism, judgmentalism, rejection, politics, and science were the main barriers to Christianity for this group of Nones.

THE CHRISTIANS IN YOUR DAILY LIFE

The conversation stretched enthusiastically late into the night. Toward the end, I asked, "You guys tell me what you think about this, but I think there is a broad stereotype of Christians socially, politically, culturally, and then there is the idea of Christians in your everyday life and your experience of them. And some of those are consistent, and some of those are inconsistent. But I'd love to hear your thoughts about the Christians in your life. What do you think about them as people, as human beings?"

Alice was the first to reply: "I have several friends now who really identify with the faith and practice regularly . . . some of whom I've known for a really long time and have a nostalgic familiarity with, but others who are relatively new, and it's really refreshing to me to see people who are really authentic with their faith."

Claire concurred, saying, "Both my mother and Katherine, who is one of my best friends, are very strong in their faith, and I admire that. And I'm sometimes envious of it because I've tried to get there and I can't. So I very much would not make the conclusion [that all Christians] . . . fulfill that stereotype of hypocrisy because I've found that not to be true in my real life."

Crista also indicated envy toward Christians. "One of the things that makes me envious of people who are religious is that they have an automatic community . . . they have this shared value that brings them together on a weekly basis or a yearly basis if they go to church at Christmas, and I don't have that." She continued, "Nones are the people who are not religious, and they don't go to church every week or worship, and we don't have space to talk about . . . we don't have that shared value that might lead us to other people who feel the same way we do. Sort of the way that friendship naturally develops. Because you don't have a group for an absence of a thought or an absence of a belief. That doesn't exist."

"There is no real community," Crista summarized, "for unbelief." The rest of the group agreed.

Strangely, though they despised Christianity as a stereotype, they appreciated the character of many Christians they knew and the community those Christians enjoyed.

As our time together drew to a close and we all started gathering our things to leave, I asked one final, personal question: "Unlike all of you, I did not grow up in a practicing Christian home, and yet I am raising my daughters in a home that practices Christianity. How do I do so in such a way they will not walk away from the faith? What is your advice for me?" This group of atheists and agnostics told me to give them room and freedom to ask questions and not to dismiss their questions with easy answers.

I expected a degree of hesitancy among atheists and agnostics to discuss religion, but as I learned later, their conversation lingered into the night, long after I had departed.

THE KALEO PROJECT

Based on my research, my "walk though Athens," and my conversations with these fifteen young adults, my colleague Dr. Betsy Wagner and I selected churches to participate in the Kaleo Project, the first phase of the Young Adult Initiative. In New Testament Greek, *kaleo* means "to call, to invite." Where can the Nones be found in the Denver metro area? How can churches in the Denver area call out to them, inviting them into life-giving relationships? This was the focus and the mission of the Kaleo Project, Denver Seminary's arm of the Lilly Endowment's Young Adult Initiative. In 2016, the Lilly Endowment generously and thoughtfully funded this grant in order to help "congregations understand that they must listen to the desires and hopes of young adults today and identify barriers that may discourage or unintentionally block young people from participating."[8]

To secure as many applications as possible, I advertised through the Denver Seminary network and publications, met with pastors associated with Denver Seminary, and personally called for applications multiple times on three separate Christian radio stations in the Denver metro area. From our pool of more than fifty applicants, we selected eighteen churches. Betsy and I consulted maps of the Denver metro area and the demographics of each applicant to ensure not

---

8. "Reaching Young Adults," Lilly Endowment Inc., accessed February 21, 2021, lillyendowment.org/reaching-young-adults-build-new-ministries/.

only that they had thought carefully about their passion and plan to reach the Nones but also that the pool of churches was diverse in age, denomination, racial makeup, and geographical location. Each church that participated in the project received a $30,000 grant distributed over three years. These funds enabled them to innovate, create, and break from weathered ministry approaches that are no longer effective in today's culture. In turn, we walked alongside these churches and listened to their struggles, their stories, and their questions.

Each semester for three years (fall, spring, and summer), a trained member of my research team (comprised of Denver Seminary students) was assigned to up to three or four of the participating churches. They would attend these churches and observe young adult events, interview at least twenty young adults or young adult leaders, and conduct one focus group per semester. The purpose was to discover the challenges and triumphs of leaders who minister to young adults, to understand the lives and concerns of young adults, and to document what types of outreach were most effective. Our team of researchers met twice monthly to discuss our findings and troubleshoot any concerns or difficulties. At the end of each semester, each researcher compiled a report based on their findings, along with the transcripts of each interview and focus group. In the end, our team conducted more than five hundred interviews, more than one hundred focus groups, and more than ten thousand pages of data.

QUESTIONS FOR INDIVIDUAL AND SMALL GROUP REFLECTION

1. Why do you think so many atheists and agnostics were willing to discuss God and Christianity?
2. What surprised you most about what the focus group said?

3. Have you ever personally asked the questions they posed? If so, how did you resolve them and what was left unresolved?

4. Why do you think they despised Christianity as a whole, but when asked to describe Christians they knew, they described them in glowing terms?

5. What are the most important things we should do to repair the reputation of the church?

6. In what other ways or places do young adults seek spirituality apart from the church?

7. Do you think there is a community for unbelief? Why or why not?

8. What do you think of the group's advice on how to raise a child who will not depart from the faith?

9. Should Christians be involved in politics? If so, to what extent? If not, why not?

10. How could the gospel comfort the participant who said, "And also, we're not the center of the universe; we're actually really far off to a side. I mean, we're actually less than a speck of dust"?

THREE

THE WHO

*Young Adults in the
Twenty-First Century*

May you live in interesting times.
—Sir Austen Chamberlain, 1936

Y ou ladies going all the way up?" the man asked, sweat beading
around his temples and victory gleaming in his eyes. He had just
picked his way down through the rock scramble from the summit of
Quandary Peak near Breckenridge, Colorado. I glanced at my daughters, who were resting on a nearby boulder. Smiling, I nodded. "I don't
know if you'll make it," he cautioned. "Storms." The weatherperson
that morning had said the same: be off the mountain by noon.

It was standard advice for anyone hoping to scale a fourteener—a
fourteen-thousand-foot peak—on a sunny Colorado summer day. But
growing up in the country before the internet, Siri, Alexa, and smartwatches has its advantages. On most days, I can read the weather in the

clouds and the wind. Climbing a fourteener was an annual tradition for me and my daughters, and the clouds belied all the predictions. The girls and I continued on, summiting the mountain safely.

Weather forecasts are based on statistical models that combine data collected from satellites, barometers, radars, weather balloons, and other instruments located on land, in the water, and in the atmosphere. They describe current weather conditions and make predictions about the future. Sometimes, just as the man's weather prediction contradicted my own that day on Quandary Peak, statistical predictions contradict one another. Even before the plethora of weather apps that contradict one another, weatherpeople have long been criticized for being wrong.

We use statistics to understand the world around us—in medicine, business, science, politics, and consumer decisions. Statistics can measure the mood, the makeup, and even the spiritual health of a nation. For many years, we have relied on statistics to understand the Nones without input from psychological development or the grander sociological story. But to shape these generations of Nones, we must understand not only the major events that shaped their worldview but also how those things differ from the events that shaped the worldview of every other living generation.

LOOKING AT THE TUMULTUOUS
CULTURE THAT SHAPED US

To shape the world, we must first understand how the world is shaping us. From the moment we are born, the world—our culture, our family, the conditions in which we live—presses in on us, molding our views, our values, and to a degree, even our personalities. Under the best circumstances, these influences shape us into people capable of meeting the challenges of our time.

Yet the agitated quaking of recent seismic cultural shifts has left even the most learned and wisest among us grappling for understanding. Where are we, how did we get here, and where we are headed? Who among us was prepared? Who was raised for the world we find ourselves in today? The first two decades of the twenty-first century were marked by dramatic and shocking events that changed the way we thought about politics, religion, and the world. At the dawn of this new millennium, on September 11, 2001, a total of 2,996 people were killed in terrorist attacks in New York City, Washington, DC, and a field in Somerset County, Pennsylvania. On October 7, 2001, the United States, with British support, officially launched Operation Enduring Freedom—what would ultimately be America's longest war to date—with air strikes on al-Qaeda and Taliban forces. On March 19, 2003, the war expanded to another front with Operation Iraqi Freedom.

On August 29, 2005, Category 3 hurricane Katrina made landfall in Louisiana near Buras-Triumph. Hurricane Katrina and its aftermath claimed more than 1,800 lives and became the costliest disaster in US history. In December 2007, the emergence of subprime mortgage losses led to a global economic downturn that rivaled the Great Depression. In 2013, three female black activists launched the Black Lives Matter movement in response to the acquittal of George Zimmerman, who shot and killed an unarmed black youth named Trayvon Martin.

In 2016, businessman and amateur politician Donald Trump bested experienced candidate Hillary Clinton in the presidential election. On October 1, 2017, Stephen Paddock opened fire on a country music festival from the thirty-second floor of the Mandalay Bay Resort and Casino in Las Vegas, Nevada, killing fifty-eight people and wounding more than eight hundred. It was the deadliest shooting in US history at the time of the attack. And on January 9, 2020, the World Health Organization announced a mysterious coronavirus-related illness originating in Wuhan, China—a plague that ultimately brought the world to its knees.

Like an undulating tide that shapes the shoreline, these events have shaped us, transforming the way we understand ourselves, our families, our nation, and our world. The way these events shaped us depended largely on our vantage point—our ethnicity, gender, economic health, mental health, spiritual health, and physical health—but it also depended on our generation and the season of life in which we found ourselves during these events.

TALKIN' 'BOUT OUR GENERATIONS

The eldest among us, born roughly between 1928 and 1945, survived the Great Depression and a world war that claimed the lives of an estimated seventy-five million people around the world. They are perhaps the most prepared for the civil and economic unrest unfurling around the globe. And yet this generation, the silent generation, was raised in a world without televisions and, in many cases, without electricity. My nanny, born on the plains of West Texas in 1932, often regales us with tales of her childhood spent gathered around the radio listening to Fibber McGee and Molly or running to fetch water from the well when it came time to wash dishes. Her father bought a car with a rumble seat when she was three or four years old, and when the harsh winds of a West Texas winter froze the windshield, they thawed it with an onion. When I hear her stories, it is the quiet I hear most: the absence of the "noise" of modern-day life—twenty-four-seven media, phone notifications, the steady rush of ground traffic, air traffic, and sirens.

The birth of the first baby boomers coincided with the world's first-deployed atomic bomb, when an American B-29 bomber dropped an A-bomb over the city of Hiroshima on August 6, 1945. Three days later, a second B-29 dropped another atomic bomb over Nagasaki.

Having survived great hardships and instability, the silent generation sought to provide stability and economic prosperity for their children, the boomers. Thus the boomers witnessed an economic and fertility boom born on the backs of their hardworking parents. Demographers William Strauss and Neil Howe comment, "Returning vets [from World War II] wanted to get married, have kids, and move into nice homes and productive jobs."[1] The silent generation urged their children to do the same. My own grandfather, a cotton farmer, strenuously urged his children to obtain a college education so their livelihoods would not "depend so perilously upon the weather." Each of his children received a college education as well as most of his grandchildren.

The baby boomers' childhoods were marked by stratospheric optimism. It was "an era when large institutions were regarded as effective, government as powerful, science as benign, schools as good, careers as reliable, families as strong, and crime as under control."[2] But the optimism of Pax Americana,[3] memorialized in Norman Rockwell paintings and vintage television, buckled in 1963 with the assassination of John F. Kennedy. The boomers' key developmental years did not necessarily prepare them for the financial and civil instability of the world today.

America's "neglected middle child,"[4] Generation X (comprised of about sixty-five million people), is dwarfed by the size of the preceding generation (approximately seventy-seven million baby boomers) and the following generation (approximately eighty-three million

---

1. William Strauss and Neil Howe, *The Fourth Turning: An American Prophecy—What the Cycles of History Tell Us About America's Next Rendezvous with Destiny* (New York: Broadway Books, 1997), 146.

2. Ibid., 147. These descriptions are generalizations of an era and should not be construed to include the experience of all peoples, especially minorities and other marginalized people.

3. Pax Americana, also popularly known as "Good Times," "Happy Days," or "American High," is defined by the *Oxford International Encyclopedia of Peace* (2010) as "a Latin phrase meaning 'American Peace' . . . describing the post World War II order."

4. Paul Taylor and George Jao, "Generation X: America's Neglected 'Middle Child,'" Pew Research Center, June 5, 2014, www.pewresearch.org/fact-tank/2014/06/05/generation-x-americas-neglected-middle-child/.

millennials), which often leads them to be overlooked in popular culture. Their childhoods (having been born between 1965 and 1980) coincided with the social and sexual revolutions of the 1960s and 1980s. Skyrocketing divorce rates and more opportunities for women in the workplace led to exploding anxiety over these children returning to empty homes after school, thus ladening them with the term "latchkey kids." Drs. Thomas and Lynette Long interviewed more than three hundred elementary school children who returned to empty homes and "documented serious problems of anxiety, fears, loneliness and depression among elementary school children who spend substantial blocks of time alone at home in the mornings or afternoons while their parents work."[5]

The collective experiences of Generation X created an extraordinarily resilient cohort. Left to their own devices from an early age, they developed into independent, self-reliant, and self-sufficient individuals. They were also known to be skeptical of authority and large institutions. I am a "cusper," born in 1978 at the end of one generation and the dawn of another. I share many of the traits attributed to Generation X: a latchkey kid with divorced parents, self-reliant (to a fault), and skeptical about the trustworthiness of government and large institutions. However, my two younger brothers are millennials, and my first memory of a world news event was the fall of the Berlin Wall, hailed a triumph of Western civilization.

Although it could be surmised that the skepticism of Gen Xers prepared them for a chaotic world of competing metanarratives, in their lifetimes they have grappled with unprecedented technological growth and expansion. When they were children, they watched the space adventures of Captain Kirk in *Star Trek*; as adults, they watched Captain Kirk (i.e., William Shatner) launch into space aboard a Blue Origin New Shephard rocket.

---

5. Judy Mann, "The Lives of Latchkey Children," *Washington Post*, November 29, 1985, www.washingtonpost.com/archive/local/1985/11/29/the-lives-of-latchkey-children/12712d60 -ee0a-4844-a4ce-740bf0eaf3f9/.

Millennials were born in an age of optimism about the stability of Western civilization. They believed they could make a difference and build a meaningful life. American millennials (and their parents) shared the view of Lin-Manuel Miranda's character Alexander Hamilton in the hit Broadway musical *Hamilton*: "America, you great unfinished symphony, you sent for me. You let me make a difference—a place where even orphan immigrants can leave their fingerprints and rise up."[6]

Unlike Gen Xers, millennials were born in a time when children were no longer "seen as a hindrance to their parents' social or professional development; now they were seen as the pinnacle of their parents' development—something chosen, desired, and representative of all their other life efforts."[7] Millennials were raised by "helicopter parents" who awarded participation trophies and sought to protect them from hardship. They grew up believing certain promises:

1. If you are willing to work hard and go to college, you can have the nice home with the white picket fence, a happy marriage, 2.5 kids, and a dog.
2. It is okay to take out student loans for college because, ultimately, you will find a job that will help you repay those student loans.
3. This job will provide security through health insurance for your family and future financial stability through retirement programs.
4. Women can have it all: fulfilling careers and successful, satisfying family lives.

---

6. "The World Was Wide Enough," *Hamilton*, music and lyrics by Lin-Manuel Miranda, directed by Thomas Kail (New York: Richard Rodgers Theatre, June 2016), aired July 3, 2020, on Disney+.

7. Elisabeth A. Nesbit Sbanotto and Craig L. Blomberg, *Effective Generational Ministry: Biblical and Practical Insights for Transforming Church Communities* (Grand Rapids, MI: Baker Academic, 2016), 170.

Though millennials are more at home with technology than their predecessors, they were not raised for the world as it is today. With the subprime mortgage crisis and subsequent recession in 2008, the promises upon which they were raised were dashed. Millennials graduated from college into the worst economy since the Great Depression. Homes were unaffordable, jobs—along with the security they provided in the past—were scarce, and the precarious "gig economy" was born. Women discovered that, yes, they could have it all—just not all at the same time. Even before the COVID-19 pandemic led to 1.8 million women leaving the workforce[8], many millennial women were questioning the value of a life strained by the pressures of both work and family.

One of the youngest generations among us,[9] Generation Z, was born into a world rife with political tension, social upheaval, economic instability, and rapid technological innovation. Born between 1996 and 2012, this generation has no substantive memory of a world without war or smartphones. As the first digital natives, the whole, fiery, burning world has always been at their fingertips. Thus, Gen Zs, like the silent generation, tend to be pragmatic, seeking jobs and lifestyles that provide stability and security. This generation is the most racially and ethnically diverse in America, with a bare majority (52 percent) identifying as non-Hispanic white.[10]

The youngest of Generation Z is, at the time of this writing, still coming of age, and much is left to learn about them, their views, and

---

8. Matt Gonzales, "Nearly Two Million Fewer Women in Labor Force," SHRM, February 17, 2022, www.shrm.org/resourcesandtools/hr-topics/behavioral-competencies/global-and-cultural-effectiveness/pages/over-1-million-fewer-women-in-labor-force.aspx.

9. Currently labeled Generation Alpha, the youngest generation is the group of people born after 2012. Since this generation is still so young, few meaningful studies have been conducted to shed light on its characteristics and how Generation Alpha might influence world events.

10. Kim Parker and Ruth Igielnik, "On the Cusp of Adulthood and Facing an Uncertain Future: What We Know About Gen Z So Far," Pew Research Center, May 14, 2020, www.pewresearch.org/social-trends/2020/05/14/on-the-cusp-of-adulthood-and-facing-an-uncertain-future-what-we-know-about-gen-z-so-far-2/.

their defining traits. Among all living generations, Generation Z and Generation Alpha, born from 2010 to the 2020s, will perhaps be best prepared to meet the challenges of our time. In my own home, many world events floor me while my daughters, born in 2009 and 2011, find them par for the course. Like most others, when COVID-19 sent the world into lockdown, I was shocked by the events unfurling around me. A pandemic? A contagious, deadly disease for which we had no medicine? Was this not the twenty-first century? (Clearly, I had not read enough dystopian literature yet. Consider that now sorted.) But for my daughters, these events were at first a novelty (no school!) and then an inconvenience. At no point did they display the same surprise or shock I did. At one point, after unwisely viewing the news about the mounting number of COVID-19 deaths, the political and civil unrest, and the fraility of the economy, I muttered to myself, "This is so not normal." My daughters, bat ears attuned, replied, "Of course it is normal, in a way." I realized then that, born on the heels of the 2008 financial crisis with a twenty-year war raging in the Middle East, they had never known a time of peace or economic stability.

But like many in my generation, I had. I had been born in a pause.

BEING BORN IN A PAUSE

Every generation must enter the season of adulthood, when we, as the apostle Paul urges in 1 Corinthians 13:11, "put the ways of childhood" behind us (NIV). Every generation must come of age, but not every generation comes of age on September 11, 2001 or in September 2008 at the beginning of the Great Recession, as happened with millennials and the youngest Gen Xers, the eldest of the Nones.

The events of the early aughts cleaved our lives in half—there was the life we knew before, promises in hand, and the life we knew after, promises shattered, future unknown.

In a joint production of the BBC and HBO, writer and producer

Russell T. Davies captures the angst of late Gen Xers and millennials. The drama *Years and Years* explores the near future through the day-to-day lives of the Lyons family. Following a blistering montage of twenty-four-seven world news events, the Lyons siblings share a meal of Chinese takeaway and discuss world events in light of their childhood.

> **Stephen:** Tell you what's weird, though. Do you remember years ago? We used to think the news was boring.
> **Daniel:** Oh my God, golden days! The news would come on and we would just yawn.
> **Stephen:** Now we hide. I have to hide my eyes, literally.
> **Evelyn:** It's like at school when they'd tell you about the olden days, with Sun Kings and people electing pigs. It's coming back. It's happening again.
> **Stephen:** We were lucky for a bit, born in the '80s. We had like thirty years. The first thirty years of our lives.
> **Evelyn:** Couple of wars.
> **Stephen:** Yeah, all right. But you and me, we had a nice time. Basically, we had a really nice time. Turns out, we were born in a pause.[11]

On the morning of the 9/11 terrorist attacks, I was reading Habakkuk between calls at a crisis hotline. When I heard the news of American Airlines Flight 11 hitting the North Tower, I was reading Habakkuk 1:2–3:

> O LORD, how long shall I cry for help,
>> and you will not hear?
> Or cry to you "Violence!"
>> and you will not save?

---

11. *Years and Years*, season 1, episode 4, directed by Simon Cellan Jones, aired June 4, 2019, on BBC One, 6:51, play.hbomax.com/player/urn:hbo:episode:GXN7iKwaagcLDwgEAAAPJ .

Why do you make me see iniquity,
>and why do you idly look at wrong?
Destruction and violence are before me;
>strife and contention arise.

I did not yet understand the magnitude of the events unfolding in New York, nor how the words of this minor prophet from the seventh century BC were crashing into my life as I read them.

When United Airlines Flight 175 crashed into the South Tower, I was reading Habakkuk 2:1:

I will take my stand at my watchpost
>and station myself on the tower,
and look out to see what he will say to me,
>and what I will answer concerning my complaint.

When the towers fell, I read from Habakkuk 3:2 and prayed with the prophet:

O Lord, I have heard the report of you,
>and your work, O Lord, do I fear.
In the midst of the years revive it;
>in the midst of the years make it known;
>in wrath remember mercy.

I was twenty-three years old when the towers fell. Paul and I had been married for two months. When the towers fell, so, too, did my vision, my best hopes, for what my future with Paul would look like, for the family we would one day have, for the kind of world our children would inhabit. I, like others in my generational cohort as well as millennials, had been born and raised in a pause, and now the world whirled on again, playing the same dirge it had from time immemorial.

Sometimes I find myself homesick for a world that no longer exists. My family still lives on the country property where I was raised, and I can go back to Texas. I can go back to the country, to blacktop roads lined with honeysuckle vines and shortleaf pines. I can go back to the one-stoplight town, to the Friday-night lights. I can go back to the nineteenth-century building that was once a mercantile for pioneers but is now my family's antique mall. But I cannot go back to the world as it was before 9/11, before the internet, smartphones, social media, and twenty-four-seven news. Nor can any of us.

We live in interesting times, and the events of the preceding two decades have not given us reason to expect any different in the years to come. As J. R. R. Tolkien expressed on the heels of World War II through his character Frodo, "'I wish it need not have happened in my time,' said Frodo. 'So do I,' said Gandalf, 'and so do all who live to see such times. But that is not for them to decide.'"[12] The English expression, "May you live in interesting times," is of obscure provenance, and though it sounds like a blessing, it is really a curse. I wish we lived in more mundane times. I wish we could press the pause button once again. But in this, we do not get a choice. As Gandalf ultimately instructs Frodo, "All we have to decide is what to do with the time that is given us."[13]

LIVING NOT WITHOUT PAIN BUT WITHOUT STAIN

Those born in a pause are the summer children who have never known a winter. Now, as adults, we grapple with a very different world than the one we knew as we grew and developed into adults. For this reason, it may be harder for those born and raised in a pause to fully

12. J. R. R. Tolkien, *The Lord of the Rings* (London: HarperCollins, 1991), 64.
13. Ibid.

understand and appreciate the chaotic and unpredictable world that younger generations must navigate. Young adults often express frustration with their baby boomer or older Gen X parents, stating, "They just don't understand how hard it is to get a secure job or afford a home anymore."

Statistics provide us with a bird's-eye view of everything from weather to what may be happening with younger generations. Sociological story gives us context, texture, and empathy from one generation to the next. There was one prognosticator who was never wrong. Though Jesus' sinless life and death on the cross afforded believers lives of forgiveness and freedom from sin, we will not be without pain. In John chapter 16, Jesus described the future his disciples could expect. He told them to expect great sorrow but also great joy. He explained that in the world they would have θλῖψιν (*thlipsin*), rendered "tribulation" in the English Standard Version (v. 33). The Greek word *thlipsin* means constriction, rubbing together, a narrow place of no escape. No matter our generation, we can expect *thlipsin*, which will one day turn to joy. All we must do now is decide what to do in our time, in our communities, in our churches, in our neighborhoods, in our homes, and in our lives. May we all do this with wisdom and discernment, equipped with knowledge of Scripture and how it applies to our times.

QUESTIONS FOR INDIVIDUAL AND SMALL GROUP REFLECTION

1. What cultural factors or world events do you think are driving the rise of the Nones?
2. Should the fact that the Nones were identified first in 1968, not in 2011, change the way we think about this group? Why or why not?

3. Do you agree that Nones are a weather vane that is showing us the direction the nation is headed? Why or why not?

4. If you are a believer, are there any beliefs you share with the Nones (e.g., the church is too political, etc.)? If so, which ones and why?

5. In what ways do you think the environment you grew up in shaped who you are today?

6. What factors (such as your culture, family, or faith) do you think most impacted who you are today?

7. Which events of the first two decades of the twenty-first century have influenced you the most? Why? How did these events influence you?

8. In what ways are you similar to your generational cohort? In what ways are you different?

9. What effect do you think "growing up in a pause" might have had on the development and coming of age of the eldest Nones?

10. What tools have you found most useful in helping you apply Scripture to your culture or life circumstances?

FOUR

THE WHEN

Understanding the Times

> *These are the numbers of the divisions of the*
> *armed troops who came to David in Hebron to*
> *turn the kingdom of Saul over to him, according*
> *to the word of the LORD. . . . Of Issachar,*
> *men who had understanding of the times, to*
> *know what Israel ought to do, 200 chiefs, and*
> *all their kinsmen under their command.*
> —1 Chronicles 12:23, 32

In times of chaos and crisis, the people who rise to lead are some-times those we least expect. On his deathbed, Jacob proclaimed over his son Issachar:

> Issachar is a strong donkey,
> crouching between the sheepfolds.

41

He saw that a resting place was good,
and that the land was pleasant,
so he bowed his shoulder to bear,
and became a servant at forced labor.

—Genesis 49:14–15

They settled in the center of the promised land, a fertile valley bordered by Manasseh, Zebulun, and Naphtali.

We know very little about the tribe of Issachar, but we know they were both tradesmen and scholars, working with their hands and their heads, acquainted with both difficult labor and the study of the Torah. In the great war between the house of David and the house of Saul recorded in 2 Samuel, it was not the Levites, the priestly class, that directed Israel on what they should do but rather the tribe of Issachar. The Bible describes the men of Issachar as "men who had understanding of the times, to know what Israel ought to do" (1 Chron. 12:32).

No one, not even the very learned or wise, can foresee the future. But to understand how we, as Christians, can faithfully fulfill our calling in this cultural moment, we must prayerfully seek to develop cultural intelligence to understand our times. We must prayerfully understand not only who we are and how world events have affected us but also the powerful undercurrents of the culture in which we live. As Darrell Bock writes in his book *Cultural Intelligence: Living for God in a Diverse, Pluralistic World*, "Cultural intelligence requires that we understand what is happening around us and how to engage these changes well."[1] Mirroring the militaristic language from 1 Chronicles, Bock asks, "Has the church's approach to doing battle been effectively defined and practiced? Have we missed the exact nature of the battle and misdirected our mission?"[2]

---

1. Darrell L. Bock, *Cultural Intelligence: Living for God in a Diverse, Pluralistic World* (Nashville: B&H Academic, 2020), 1.
2. Ibid.

From the day the towers fell, my personal prayer has centered on 1 Chronicles 12:32. I long for the discernment to understand the times in which we live. I yearn for the wisdom to know how I and my fellow believers can respond faithfully. What are the unique challenges of our time? What is needed for such a time as this?

CHRISTIANITY AND CULTURE

The crystalline sand shore and turquoise waters of Panama City Beach are among the most beautiful in the world. While vacationing with my family one summer during college, I grew enchanted with the undersea world created by the two sandbars that run parallel to the coast. The space between the two sandbars forms a "highway" for diverse marine life. Every day, the white sands burned underfoot as I crossed the beach to submerse myself in a rainbowed world of gold, red, green, and blue schools of fish. Sea turtles and jellyfish skittered along the sea floor, and pods of dolphins gleefully cavorted along this marine highway.

These dual sandbars also create dangerous riptides that make Panama City Beach one of the deadliest beaches in America. The key to safety is to know the tide, monitor changes in the currents, and check the shore frequently for changes in the riptide flag system. Despite my training and experience as a lifeguard (or perhaps *because* of them), after a few days, my vigilance flagged one afternoon, and the riptide carried me out to sea, far past the second sandbar. With a deep knowledge of my own smallness compared to the great gravitational forces of the sun and moon upon the ocean, I peacefully held my breath and let the tide carry me until it released me back to the surface. The first rule of survival is not to panic. I did not fight the tide because I knew I *could not* fight the tide.

Culture is not too different from swimming in the Gulf of Mexico. We are all swimming in one culture and many different subcultures, whether we wish to or not, and living outside the influence of *any* culture is as likely as a pod of dolphins living on dry land. Culture is a great force, a group of people's way of life, comprised of their knowledge, traditions, religion, cuisine, customs, and arts.

The proper relationship between Christianity and culture has been argued and debated since the early Christians sought to discern how to live within Roman and Jewish contexts. From the dawn of Christianity, the tenets of the Christian faith were decidedly at odds with the surrounding culture. Down through the centuries, this alone has remained constant: the order of culture and society has always been at odds with the principles of the Christian faith.

What relationship, then, should Christians have with the surrounding culture? Should Christians reject any culture outside the church? Should we embrace it? Should we seek to transform it? In his 1951 book, *Christ and Culture*, theologian Reinhold Niebuhr reminds us, "The question of Christianity and civilization is by no means a new one; that Christian perplexity in this area has been perennial, and that the problem has been an enduring one through all the Christian centuries."[3]

Part of the difficulty in discerning our task lies in understanding what "culture" means. The term *culture* is rooted in the idea of *cultivation*, like agriculture. "For centuries," writes Austrian psychologist Gustav Jahoda, "[culture] meant producing or developing something,

---

3. Reinhold Niebuhr, *Christ and Culture* (1951; repr, New York: HarperCollins, 2001), 2. In his book, he outlines five approaches the church (and/or Christianity) can have with culture: (1) Christ against Culture, in which Christians radically break from culture, (2) Christ of Culture, in which culture is accepted and celebrated with little or no critique, (3) Christ above Culture, in which culture is basically good but needs Christian refinement, (4) Christ and Culture in Paradox, in which Christians accept the authority of both Christ and culture in tension, and (5) Christ the Transformer of Culture, in which culture is believed originally good but corrupted through the fall and Christians ought to work toward transformation of the culture. In the ensuing seventy years, people have disputed and outright refuted these five categories, but they have served as the basecamp from which many theologians, philosophers, and other Christian thinkers have explored other ways of defining the appropriate relationship between Christianity and culture.

such as 'the culture of barley' or 'the culture of the arts' and is still employed in this sense as in 'culture of bacteria.'"[4]

Only in eighteenth-century France was the term first used as a noun, in the sense of "training or refinement of the mind or taste," then quickly thereafter, "the qualities of an educated person" knowledgeable about the world.[5] Today, when discussing the relationship between Christianity and culture, we often mean "the customary beliefs, social forms, and material traits of a racial, religious, or social group."[6]

Whatever culture or subculture we live in, our faith compels us to reject some aspects (e.g., pornography or love of money), transform others (e.g., homelessness, drug abuse and addiction, human trafficking), and embrace others (e.g., freedom, equality, racial and ethnic diversity). The most difficult aspects to grapple with are those that can be used for good or evil, such as, most notably for our current conversation, technology. The appropriate use of technology can be difficult to discern because it appears to be morally neutral.

TECHNOLOGICAL PROGRESS

The twenty-first century, a mere two decades old, has brought more changes than many of our ancestors witnessed in their lifetimes. As author Thomas Friedman stated in an address to the 2017 Resnick Aspen Action Forum, "We forget you could go a whole century without your bow and arrow getting better. There was no bow-and-arrow 2.0 between the eleventh and twelfth centuries."[7] There were, of course, periodic breakthroughs, bright spots, and brilliant minds.

---

4. Gustav Jahoda, "Critical Reflections on Some Recent Definitions of 'Culture,'" *Culture and Psychology* 18, no. 3 (2012): 289–90, doi.org/10.1177/1354067X12446229.

5. Ibid. 290.

6. *Merriam-Webster Dictionary*, s.v., "culture," accessed September 17, 2021, www.merriam-webster.com/dictionary/culture.

7. Thomas Friedman, "Closing Lunch: In Conversation with Tom Friedman," Resnick Aspen Action Forum 2017 (Aspen, CO: Aspen Meadows, July 31, 2017), video shared live

In 1450, Johannes Gutenberg commercially introduced his printing press to the world. Polymath and acclaimed painter Leonardo da Vinci (1452–1519), whose works include *The Last Supper*, also made significant scientific contributions in the areas of engineering, anatomy, and physiology. In 1543, Copernicus triggered the Scientific Revolution with his book, *De revolutionibus orbium coelestium* (*On the Revolutions of the Heavenly Spheres*), in which he posited the sun, not the earth, was the center of the universe. In 1609, heavily influenced by the work of Copernicus, Galileo built the first telescope, which led him to observe that the earth circled the sun.

And yet, even the significant contributions of the collective scientific revolutions in our history cannot compete with the pace of change we are witnessing today. The last three decades have brought an incredible diversity of life-altering inventions, including the worldwide web (1989, the most recognized form of the internet), mobile broadband (1991), email and text messaging (1992), GPS for civilians (1993), Netflix (1997), Google Search (1998), MP3 players (1997), the Toyota Prius (1997), the International Space Station (1998), human embryonic stem cells (1998), tools to support the completed Human Genome Project (2003), Facebook (2004), YouTube (2005), the iPhone (2007), the Tesla Roadster (2008), the gene-editing tool CRISPR (2012), and the first all-civilian space flight (2021).

Historians and futurists alike disagree on whether such technological progress will continue to multiply to the point of technological singularity, a hypothetical future point at which technology will become uncontrollable and irreversible. Regardless, technology has changed the way we live, work, educate, and entertain ourselves. We find, build, and sustain relationships at great distances. We have access to a limitless supply of information. We have improved access to healthcare and improved patient outcomes. We keep ourselves and our

by The Aspen Institute, on YouTube, 45:53, www.youtube.com/watch?v=UmMPpq9PwGg&ab_channel=TheAspenInstitute.

loved ones safer with GPS tracking apps, wireless security alarms, and low-cost doorbell security cameras. Many kept their jobs (and their social sanity) during a worldwide pandemic through virtual meetings.

Yet technology is a powerful riptide in our culture, carrying many (but especially young adults)[8] away from spiritual, mental, emotional, physical, and even fiscal health. One of the most surprising findings in our research for the Kaleo Project was just how cynical young adults are about technology and the impact it is having on their lives. If we want to help young adults—not just engage them—and if we indeed want to *minister to* them, we must vigilantly seek to understand the impact technology is having on them. As one young adult from a focus group, Justin, noted, "We live in a generation where not only is the spoken word available at a touch but also people's faces. Straight-up FaceTime. We have instant access to everything. We are not, obviously, prepared for this, it's not just our generation . . . I don't think anyone on the planet was prepared for what's happened."

Though young adults are struggling in numerous ways, many of which we will cover in the coming chapters, one thread woven throughout each of them is the impact technology has on their daily lives because of the acceleration of cultural change.

THREE KEY ISSUES WITH TECHNOLOGY

In a speech to the House of Lords on October 28, 1943, Sir Winston Churchill stated, "We shape our buildings and afterwards our buildings shape us."[9] The same could be said of any tools we create. Contrary to what one may expect, young adults today (especially those

8. Ursula Oberst et al., "Negative Consequences from Heavy Social Networking in Adolescents: The Mediating Role of Fear of Missing Out," *Journal of Adolescence* 55, no. 1 (February 2017): doi.org/10.1016/j.adolescence.2016.12.008.

9. Winston Churchill, "House of Commons Rebuilding" (meeting with the House of Lords, London, October 28, 1943), api.parliament.uk/historic-hansard/commons/1943/oct /28/house-of-commons-rebuilding.

in Generation Z) have several deep concerns about how technological tools are affecting their lives and characters.

First, many young adults we spoke with expressed dismay over how instant gratification afforded by technology has led to what they believe are character deficits. In one focus group, four friends in their twenties discussed how technology has affected their attention spans:

> **Amber:** There's so much right in your hand, which is awesome in some ways, but also just so distracting in others, because you have everything—way more than what you would have naturally thought of yourself—at your fingertips, and then more and more things get suggested to you, and then it's really some rabbit holes, and before you know it, you spent four hours doing who knows what instead of whatever you were supposed to be doing.
>
> **Carla:** You're like, "Oh, I'm just going to do this," but then this happened, and then this happened, and now it's midnight, and I should probably go to bed, or whatever it is.
>
> **Sarah:** And now I can't go to bed, because I'm wide awake because I had a screen in front of me.
>
> **Jen:** You also have . . . TikTok, amazing entertainment every twenty seconds; it's hilarious.
>
> **Amber:** And not even a really good movie can keep up with that!

In 1971, Nobel Prize winner Herbert A. Simon cautioned, "In an information-rich world, the wealth of information means a dearth of something else: a scarcity of whatever it is that information consumes. What information consumes is rather obvious: it consumes the attention of its recipients."[10] In other words, "a wealth of information creates a poverty of attention and a need to allocate that attention efficiently among the overabundance of information sources that might consume it."[11]

Studies back up the experiences of Amber, Carla, Sarah, and Jen as well as Herbert Simon's insights. In recent years, technology's detrimental effect on our attention spans has been vigorously debated. In 2017, the BBC reported that attention is "very much task-dependent. How much attention we apply to a task will vary depending on what the task demand is."[12] However, in 2019 scientists from Germany and Denmark published the results of a decades-long study that indicated the collective human attention span has decreased because of increased production of content across online platforms.[13] Ultimately, young adults believe this contributes to a lack of patience and undermines their abilities to interact with people face-to-face, to focus on a single task, and to perform well at work and school.

A second concern young adults have about technology is that it creates distance between themselves and previous generations. The belief that one's generation differs from that of one's parents is not unique to millennials or Gen Zs, but young adults today think technology exacerbates the divide between them and other generations. Mark, a new Christian at a nondenominational church, mentioned that with "technology changing the world faster and faster," he and his friends believe the gaps between generations have gotten steeper over the last few decades. Emily agreed, stating, "The younger generations know

---

10. Herbert A. Simon, "Designing Organizations for an Information-Rich World," chapter 2 in *Computers, Communications, and the Public Interest*, ed. Martin Greenberger (Baltimore, MD: Johns Hopkins Press, 1971), 40.

11. Ibid. 40–41.

12. Dr. Gemma Briggs, in Simon Maybin, "Busting the Attention Span Myth," BBC, March 10, 2017, www.bbc.com/news/health-38896790.

13. Philipp Lorenz-Spreen et al., "Accelerating Dynamics of Collective Attention," *Nature Communications* 10 (April 2019): www.nature.com/articles/s41467-019-09311-w.

a lot about what it means to grow up in a technologically advanced society, whereas older generations might not have that expertise."

According to the young adults I spoke with, today, a breakup means being "ghosted," photographs and videos can spread like wildfire, and embarrassing moments can live on in perpetuity. From concerns about body image to pornography to social pressure, young adults admit "a lot happens behind the screen that previous generations don't really know about." Because of this, young adults are sensitive to what they perceive to be "invalidation" by older generations: "I think there's kind of this false narrative of anything we say is almost irrelevant. It's like, 'Oh, they're just too young. They're naive.' Almost like, 'They haven't been around long enough to know that this is how it is and this is the way that it is.' When in reality, we're growing up in a very different society, in a very different culture than even our parents grew up with."

Another young adult commented, "I think we use our own experiences like a template of a journey. So [there is] this sense of, 'I thought that when I was in this stage of my life . . .' And so older generations sometimes can have a picture of what is the journey and what is maturity instead of realizing that the template they're using is not appropriate."

Young adults also described how important it is to their spiritual life that leaders understand the effects of technology, stating, "If a senior pastor is dated and doesn't understand technology quite the same way, that's a huge gap, and that's a huge struggle for people my age—just because it's super easy to become nihilistic and to think that nothing matters."

The greatest concern for young adults was what they feared to be a growing "lack of empathy" or what they called "desensitization" or "nihilism." Young adults described this in many interviews and in almost all of the twenty final focus groups. When watching the news or scrolling through updates on social media, young adults often said they "tune out," thinking, *This is too depressing,* or, *I don't care.* They are not proud of this; they simply view it as a reaction to an overload of information and their own inability to enact change.

Both men and women attributed this lack of empathy to twenty-four-seven media, online news sites, and social media trying to garner their attention by playing to their emotions. One young man, Alex, tied it back to advertising: "I think that the most negative thing that's come out of the technological explosion that's happened in the last twenty to thirty years is that now the way you make money is by getting people to click on stuff. Like, advertising is huge. Just getting people to look at stuff will have them then on your website, and then they'll buy something, right?"

Alex connected advertising methodology to the news's tactics: "I think that has completely taken over most aspects of news and stuff like that. News is no longer like, 'Hey, here's what happened.' It's like, 'Hey, let me tell you something scary,' or 'Let me tell you something that will make you angry at some other person or some other people group.' And both fear and anger can be good things, those are both things from God, but I think that the way technology has allowed the world to use fear and anger is definitely a sin."

"When you see certain images," Adam, a twenty-three-year-old, said, "like Syrian refugee children washing up, drowned, on the beach, you just go, 'Okay, I don't care. There's no point.' You're like, 'I can't do a single thing about that.'"

TECHNOLOGICAL PROGRESS VERSUS THE EVERGREEN CROSS

People from all walks of life disagree whether the positives of technological progress outweigh the negatives, and young adults are no different. Be it information overload, the distance between themselves and other generations, or a lack of empathy, young adults tend toward skepticism about the impact technology has on their daily lives, not to mention their spirituality. They view their generation as a transition or turning point in human history. As Eric, a twenty-four-year-old aerospace engineer, wisely put it, "We are [in] a digital age. And I think there's a huge tension with that with the church too. Because the church has been built on an analog world, and so I think, understandably, we're all very confused on a very deep level because there's no context for it. Our parents don't have anything to go off of; we're very much guinea pigs in a massive sociological, economic experiment. And where that ends up, I don't [know], but the answer is to hold on to Jesus. You hold on to that cross because it doesn't matter if it's analog, it doesn't matter if it's digital, that is the firmest ground—the ground of Christ."

Technology may be constantly evolving and may continue to change society for the foreseeable future, but Eric is correct: The cross is evergreen, as is humanity's need for a Savior.

This is the sociological story and cultural reality in which young adults live. We met with hundreds of young adults and young adult leaders to better understand what young adults are really, truly asking. The following chapters detail what we discovered.

QUESTIONS FOR INDIVIDUAL AND SMALL GROUP REFLECTION

1. How do you think the tribe of Issachar's identity as laborers and scholars informed their ability to discern the times and know what Israel should do?

2. Which of the five approaches to Christ and culture outlined by Niebuhr do you identify with most? Why?

3. Are there other approaches you have read of or studied that might align more closely with your views? Which ones?

4. What do you think are the top three aspects of our culture that demand Christian rejection? Why?

5. What do you think are the three aspects that most need Christian transformation?

6. In what other ways do you think the instant gratification brought about by technology is damaging to our character?

7. Do you agree that technology has widened the divide between younger and older generations? Why or why not?

8. What are the possible ramifications of a growing lack of empathy on interpersonal relationships? On society as a whole?

9. What are other "morally neutral" aspects of culture that Christians should thoughtfully consider?

10. What habits does one need to put in place to offset the potential damaging effects of technology? Why is it so difficult to put these changes in place?

PART TWO

QUESTIONS AND CHALLENGES

FIVE

QUESTION 1

Am I Alone and Unloved?

The most terrible poverty is loneliness
and the feeling of being unloved.
—Mother Teresa

High and smooth are the walls of loneliness, with no cracks or crevices by which we might scale them to escape. And loneliness lies too. It tells us no one knows us, and even if they did, they would not understand or accept us. It tells us no one is looking for us, no one values us, no one is coming for us. Loneliness is a warning signal that our relationships are deficient. The desire to be known is part of what it means to be human. In an article for *Psychology Today*, author and psychologist Dr. Gregg Henriques identifies the core psychological need of every human as "the need an individual has to be known and valued by him/herself and important others."[1]

---

1. Gregg Henriques, "The Core Need," *Psychology Today*, June 25, 2014, www.psychology today.com/us/blog/theory-knowledge/201406/the-core-need.

Yet the culture we live in, unlike the church or the Christian faith, is not poised to fulfill that longing. In the affluent West, we are beset by what Mother Teresa called "the most terrible poverty."

In January 2020, just as the world was learning of a concerning plague in Wuhan, China, the global health group Cigna released a report indicating that three in five Americans (61 percent) classify as lonely.[2] The survey, based on a national sample of 10,441 adults, revealed a 7 percent increase in loneliness over just two years. Respondents reported a number of negative mood statements, including:

1. Fifty-eight percent said they always or sometimes felt that no one knew them well.
2. More than half (52 percent) reported feeling alone sometimes or all the time.
3. Half stated they always or sometimes felt isolated from others and that their relationships with others were not meaningful.
4. Nearly half (45 percent) said they sometimes or always felt that they were no longer close to anyone.[3]

The Cigna report is just one of hundreds of studies documenting the rise of loneliness around the world. Contrary to what older generations might expect from the most technologically connected age group, the loneliest generations are also the youngest: the eldest of Generation Z, those aged eighteen to twenty-five, and millennials, aged twenty-six to forty. Connectivity is not community.

Even before the 2020 pandemic, loneliness and social isolation reached what some experts describe as epidemic proportions in the twenty-first century. As a Harvard report from 2018 puts it, "The

---

2. Cigna, *Loneliness and the Workplace: 2020 U.S. Report*, January 2020, https://www.cigna.com/static/www-cigna-com/docs/about-us/newsroom/studies-and-reports/combatting-loneliness/cigna-2020-loneliness-report.pdf.

3. Ibid., 4.

term *epidemic* is usually stamped on infectious diseases that spread across populations, but loneliness is currently impacting people in similar numbers to many public health concerns."[4]

IS SOCIAL MEDIA TRULY SOCIAL?

Why, in an age of unprecedented connectivity, when the world is at our fingertips, is loneliness on the rise? According to many psychologists and sociologists, the drivers of loneliness are social media and a lack of deep understanding about friendship.[5] The ability for us to connect with an unprecedented number of people through social media and the simultaneous increase in loneliness is a great irony. Social media impedes our ability to create and sustain meaningful friendships because it compels us to present only a curated image of our lives, blurs our understanding of what real friendships are, and channels our time away from the act of building friendships in real-world settings.

From the moment I launched a profile on Facebook on August 29, 2007, I was an avid user. The ability to connect with friends from my past and friends from a distance fascinated me. The opportunity to share my status as well as view the status of others permanently changed my view of the world. The world grew far smaller and my reach of influence much farther. After a few years, I noticed how using social media often provoked either envy or pride—two of the cardinal vices—and I worried that my usage stoked those same emotions in

---

4. Hannah Schulze, "Loneliness: An Epidemic?" *Science in the News*, Harvard University, April 16, 2018, sitn.hms.harvard.edu/flash/2018/loneliness-an-epidemic/.

5. Other drivers of loneliness are the rise of digital technology that minimizes human contact, such as the automatic checkout lanes at the grocery store compared to those lanes "hu-manned" by a person, the fragmentation of the family, busyness, and the structural changes in community. For further reading on some of these factors, read Robert Putnam's classic work, *Bowling Alone: The Collapse and Revival of American Community*.

others.[6] While these vices have always been present in my life, social media expanded the circle of who I could compare myself to. It was envy I harbored when viewing exotic vacation photos or the details of friends' new adventures. It was pride that caused me to compare myself to them in the first place. In the game of life, we want to know the score.

Comparison, of course, is as old as time. Our biblical stories, myths, and fairy tales are filled with examples. Cain jealously slaughtered his own brother, Abel, in a field when Abel's sacrifice to God was accepted but Cain's was not. The Trojan War was waged because Paris of Troy wanted Helen, the wife of the Spartan king Menelaus. The Evil Queen plotted the death of her beautiful stepdaughter, Snow White, because her beauty exceeded the queen's own. But when our circles were smaller, comparison resulted in keeping up with our neighbors. Now, our circle of comparison ostensibly can extend to any of the other 4.48 billion people who use social media,[7] and the result is a constant game of curated statuses and images. The ten major social media platforms—Facebook, YouTube, WhatsApp, Instagram, TikTok, Snapchat, Pinterest, Reddit, LinkedIn, and Twitter—are just a handful of all social media platforms, and each offers opportunities for a different type of comparison: social status, number of friends, personal attractiveness, lifestyle attractiveness, professional success, charisma, and more. On each of these platforms, we present ourselves in the best light, cropping out all that does not comport with the "image" or "brand" we want to share.

The curation of our lives means that few people truly know us. Few people know us as we are in totality—our weaknesses as well as our strengths. Curating our lives can make it difficult to be vulnerable

---

6. Not to mention 2016, in which the primary emotion could be classified as wrath. Whoops, I just mentioned it.

7. Brian Dean, "Social Network Usage and Growth Statistics: How Many People Use Social Media in 2022?" BACKLINKO, updated October 10, 2021, https://backlinko.com /social-media-users#social-media-usage-stats.

with others. We may believe that if we show our true character, others might not accept us. If no one truly knows us, what can we be but lonely? According to Cigna's survey, 58 percent of Americans feel as though no one really knows them well.[8]

Social media also blurs our understanding of what friendship is. Although we amass many "friends" on social media, research indicates there is a limit to how many friends we can have. In 1992, University of Oxford anthropologist Robin Dunbar published a study that estimated humans can know and maintain relationships with about 150 people—dubbed Dunbar's number. The two constraints limiting our social sphere? Our cognitive capabilities and the time it takes to nurture and sustain relationships.[9] In 2010, after the popularity surge of social media platforms, Dunbar revisited his research to investigate "the claim that online social environments allow us to significantly increase the size of our social networks."[10]

The study revealed three important findings:

1. Young children, and to some extent teenagers, are "poor at judging" the difference between online friends or friend requests and real relationships.
2. No matter how many "friends" one collects on social media platforms, the inner circle of meaningful relationships (identified in the study as "sympathy groups" or "support cliques") is similar to the number of offline relationships: 150.
3. Real relationships, as opposed to casual relationships, require face-to-face presence in order to maintain them.[11]

---

8. Cigna, *Loneliness and the Workplace*, 43.

9. R. I. M. Dunbar, "Neocortex Size as a Constraint on Group Size in Primates," *Journal of Human Evolution* 22, no. 6 (June 1992), doi.org/10.1016/0047-2484(92)90081-J.

10. R. I. M. Dunbar, "Do Online Social Media Cut through the Constraints That Limit the Size of Offline Social Networks?" *Royal Society Open Science* 3, no. 1 (January 2016): doi.org/10.1098/rsos.150292.

11. Ibid.

Online communities have eroded the ability of young children and teenagers to define and experience true friendship. As one article notes, "Compared with teenagers in previous decades, iGen teens are less likely to get together with their friends. They're also less likely to go to parties, go out with friends, date, ride in cars for fun, go to shopping malls or go to the movies."[12]

Without an understanding of how to build strong friendships, they may be unable to develop the skills and habits necessary to find and nurture relationships in which they know their friends and are known by their friends. While social media can expand our "connections" or "contacts," it does not expand our ability to create substantive relationships. Rather, it diminishes our ability to maintain these relationships in the real world.

WHAT IS A FRIEND?

But social media alone is not to blame for our lack of meaningful relationships. Another factor is Western culture's erosion of our understanding about friendship. We live in a culture that minimizes friendship in favor of eroticism or romantic love. Film, media, and literature celebrate romantic love but spend little time extolling the virtues of friendship. When friendship is introduced into a narrative, it is often sexualized. As viewers, we "ship" (derived from the term *relationship*) certain characters to develop a romantic attachment. When the award-winning television show *Sherlock*, starring Benedict Cumberbatch and Martin Freeman, aired in 2010, viewers began "shipping" Sherlock and Watson and speculated whether the close friendship between Sherlock and Watson was romantic. Showrunners Mark Gatiss and Steven Moffat were adamant there was no romantic

---

12. Jean Twenge, "Teens Have Less Face Time with Their Friends—and Are Lonelier Than Ever," *The Conversation*, March 20, 2019, theconversation.com/teens-have-less-face-time-with-their-friends-and-are-lonelier-than-ever-113240.

relationship between the two characters. Fans speculated that if two men lived together, worked together, and shared an emotional connection, that could only mean they were romantic partners.[13]

Even in our analog lives—our lives offline—our relationships are often diminished because we have largely lost our ability to define, recognize, and thus experience true friendships. Many studies have linked high social media usage with low development of social skills. In one study, researchers noted that "Technological Communication (internet and social media) preference strongly correlated with poor social skills and high social anxiety, while a greater restriction of technology in youth correlated in high social skills."[14] These poor social skills have given rise to several troubling behaviors regarding "romance": "textual harassment" in the workplace (sending offensive or inappropriate texts to coworkers) is on the rise,[15] "catfishing" (one person pretending to be someone they are not in order to get romantically close to the target of the affections) is prevalent, and "ghosting" (avoiding the difficult bits of ending a relationship by simply blocking a person and never contacting them again) is also on the rise.

In 1960, author and scholar C. S. Lewis noticed a dangerous tendency in confusing friendships with romantic love, writing, "It has actually become necessary in our time to rebut the theory that every firm and serious friendship is really homosexual."[16] Lewis continues, "Those who cannot conceive Friendship as a substantive love but only as a disguise or elaboration of Eros [romantic love] betray the fact that they have never had a Friend."[17]

---

13. Willa Paskin, "The Case of the Fractured Fandom," Slate, June 4, 2018, slate.com /culture /2018 /06/the-johnlock-conspiracy-sherlock-fans-disagree-with-the-shows-creators -about-holmes-and-watsons-relationship.html.

14. Prabhakararao Sampathirao, "Social Media and Social Skills," *International Journal of Indian Psychology* 3, no. 4 (July–September 2016): 57, doi.org/10.25215/0304.026.

15. Lisa A. Mainiero and Kevin J. Jones, "Sexual Harassment Versus Workplace Romance: Social Media Spillover and Textual Harassment in the Workplace," *Academy of Management Perspectives* 27, no. 3 (March 2013): journals.aom.org/doi/10.5465/amp.2012.0031.

16. C. S. Lewis, *The Four Loves* (New York, Harper Collins, 2017), 76.

17. Ibid., 76.

But what is a friend?

"To the Ancients," Lewis states, "Friendship seemed the happiest and most fully human of all loves; the crown of life and the school of virtue. The modern world, in comparison, ignores it."[18] Lewis argues that unlike agape (love of God), *storge* (love of family), and eros (romantic love), friendship is the least natural of all loves.

For Lewis, friendships are between two or more people who care about the same truth, and they are born "at the moment when one man says to another, 'What! You too? I thought that no one but myself.'"[19]

A friend is a person who knows your name. A friend knows who you are and who you are not. A friend is a fellow journeyman along the same path, with whom you can share your troubles and your burdens without fear of judgment. A friend helps you grow because they see past your defenses, denials, and blind spots. A friend celebrates with you when times are good and shows up when times are bad. A friend raises you up when you fall.

WHO REMEMBERS MY NAME?

Given the rapid acceleration of loneliness the last decade, it is not surprising that from the very beginning of the Kaleo Project, the simple act of remembering a name emerged as one of the most significant themes in our young adult research. Anne, age twenty-two, stated, "I like when people remember your name, the pastors stay in touch with you. Like want to get to know you, and it reflects in the body [of the church], too."

Emma, age twenty-four, agreed, "I think that's huge, I think that's anywhere you go. I work at a coffee shop, so if I can remember a

---

18. Ibid., 74.
19. Ibid., 99.

regular's name, that's going to make them way more open with me. So, if I'm going somewhere and someone remembers my name, that means that I matter to them, and I get plugged in."

Names have power and meaning. In his bestselling book, *How to Win Friends and Influence People*, Dale Carnegie, a self-described "simple country boy" from Missouri, notes, "Remember that a person's name is to that person the sweetest sound and most important sound in any language."[20] Carnegie further argues, "We should be aware of the magic contained in a name and realize this single item is wholly and completely owned by the person with whom we are dealing . . . and nobody else."[21]

Of course, what young adults were really expressing through the oft-repeated phrase "remember my name" was a fundamental desire to be known and to belong. Someone calling them by their name, that bright string of syllables that garners their attention throughout their lives, was an indicator that a church or church leader valued them enough to remember them.

Young adults described attending churches simply because someone remembered them, whether it was a church leader or a member of the congregation. Even if the sermon, the worship, or the church building did not particularly appeal to them, they returned to that church because they were known.

In contrast, young adults did not return to churches where they felt unknown or unseen for an extended period of time, even if they appreciated everything else about the church.

Sarah described her dismay this way: "When I first moved out to Colorado, I went to a church for over a year. I got involved in a Bible study there, and I would go to church on Sunday, and no one would know—no one knew who I was. Everyone would come up to me every week, 'Oh, is this your first week?' I'm like, 'No, I've been

---

20. Dale Carnegie, *How to Win Friends and Influence People* (New York: Gallery Books, 1981), 79.
21. Ibid., 78.

here for a year.' And so it was just like no one knew that I existed, even though I tried to be known. That makes me feel unwanted and unknown, and I did just stop going to church because I was like, 'Well, what's the point if no one's going to know who I am or check in on me?'"

"I tried to be known," Sarah said. And yet she felt unknown and even more tragically, unwanted. *Unwanted. Unwanted. Unwanted.* Her word echoed around in my head, bouncing from corner to corner like a Ping-Pong ball. To varying degrees, we all have felt unwanted at some point in our lives. What could possibly be further from our best intentions than to make a single person feel they have no place, that they, bursting with gifts and talents, are useless?

Some attributed the anonymity they felt in churches to American culture. Pedro, a recent immigrant from Mexico, explained: "When people approached to say hi . . . in the churches that I experienced while I was in seminary, it was so impersonal. No one approached me, no one asked for my name, no one. I was just one more person, and you kind of get used to it because that's the [US] culture in general. But in Mexico, at least the churches that I went to, people approach [you]. They asked for your name. They say, 'Hey, you want to grab lunch?' I was like, 'Oh, that's nice. Yeah, sure.' You know, it's just more personable."

While remembering names is important to young adults, some were content just to be recognized. In one focus group, Hannah said the warmth of leaders and church members reduced the anxiety of attending a new church: "I just think it's really important to have somebody recognize you." The simple exchange of somebody "that extends their hand and introduces [themselves], and you exchange pleasantries, and then the next week they go, 'Oh, Hannah, right?'" helped her feel seen.

Others in the group agreed.

Hannah smiled and continued, "And so, then when you sit down and you're watching the sermon or listening to the music or whatever, you already have a different perspective of it because you had that initial connection."

Aaron told of how impressed he was when someone remembered his favorite hobby. As he walked through the front doors of the church, one person said, "Hey! I remember you. You're the guy that likes to go hiking with your Siberian husky, right? Welcome back!" Though all the time and effort church leaders pour into crafting the ideal service is surely worthwhile, the single most important factor to young adults was simply being recognized and remembered.

WHAT IS IN A NAME?

"What's in a name?" William Shakespeare famously asked through Juliet Capulet. "That which we call a rose / By any other name would smell as sweet."[22] The character Juliet, if not Shakespeare himself, believed that names were of minimal importance—that the essence of an object or a person would remain the same regardless of what it was called.

While society leaves young adults with the hunger to be known and remembered, to *be wanted*, the church is perfectly poised, through its traditions and its theology, to fill that hunger. The creation narratives of Genesis reveal how important names—and the act of naming—are in the Jewish and Christian faiths. The act of naming creates order out of chaos. At the beginning of Genesis we read, "And God said, 'Let there be light,' and there was light. And God saw that the light was good. And God separated the light from the darkness. God called the light Day, and the darkness he called Night" (1:3–5).

---

22. William Shakespeare, *Romeo and Juliet*, ed. *William J. Rolfe* (New York: American Book Company, 1907), 2.2.43–44, www.google.com/books/edition/Shakespeare_s_Tragedy_of _Romeo_and_Julie/KoA0AAAAMAAJ?hl=en&gbpv=0. References are to act, scene, and line.

The word *call*, translated from the Hebrew word קָרָא (*qara*), means "to proclaim" and runs straight through the creation narratives in Genesis 1 and 2. God brought order from chaos with a word, with a name.

The first act of humankind was to name. Old Testament scholar Tremper Longman notes, "Naming is a unique ability of humanity among all of God's creatures, indicating language and the ability to categorize."[23] In Genesis 2:19, we read, "Now out of the ground the LORD God had formed every beast of the field and every bird of the heavens and brought them to the man to see what he would call them. And whatever the man called every living creature, that was its name."

God named the day, night, land, sea, and the first man,[24] but he tasked Adam with naming all other creatures, including Eve. As Adam's name was connected with his essence, meaning "from the earth," so, too, was Eve's. After God cursed the couple for eating from the forbidden tree, Adam called the woman Eve "because she was the mother of all living" (Gen. 3:20).[25]

---

23. Tremper Longman III and Scot McKnight, eds., *Genesis: The Story of God Bible Commentary* (Grand Rapids: Zondervan, 2016), 50.

24. The Hebrew word הָאָדָם, *hā-'ā-ḏām* is translated as a common name for "the man" or "man" and the proper name, Adam.

25. God changes the names of only four individuals in the Scriptures, and in each case, the new name refers to a new identity or essence. In Genesis 17, God initiates a covenant with Abram, promising that he will be "the father of a multitude of nations" (v. 4). Abram, meaning "exalted father" becomes Abraham, meaning "father of many." His wife, Sarai, meaning "my princess" becomes Sarah, "princess to many or all." The Scriptures never refer to the couple by their prior names again. Jacob, the grandson of Abraham and Sarah, is also renamed after he wrestles with God in Genesis 32. Jacob received his original name, a name meaning "he takes by the heel" or "he cheats" because his hand was holding on to his twin brother's heel at birth (Gen. 25:26). "Your name will no longer be Jacob," the unnamed man with whom he wrestles says. "You will be called Israel, because you have wrestled with God and with men, and you have won" (Gen. 32:28 CEV). The new name, יִשְׂרָאֵל (Yisrael) means "God strives." In the New Testament, when the apostle Peter correctly identifies Jesus as "the Christ, the Son of the living God," Jesus replies, "And I tell you, you are Peter, and on this rock I will build my church, and the gates of hell shall not prevail against it" (Matt. 16:16–18). Peter is derived from the Greek word *petros*, meaning "rock" or "boulder." Perhaps the most dramatic renaming in all of Scripture is that of the Pharisee Saul of Tarsus to the apostle Paul—a new name given not by God but rather by Paul himself. A common misconception is that Jesus

Throughout the Scriptures, names are bound up with a person's identity or essence. Our names are the entry point by which we are known. The name shines a torch in the darkness of anonymity, and we are seen, distinguished from others.

To be known is a core desire of all humans.

It is the duty of the church to meet that desire.

QUESTIONS FOR INDIVIDUAL AND SMALL GROUP REFLECTION

1. What do you think are the main drivers of loneliness in Western society?
2. Are you surprised by the statistics on loneliness? Why or why not?
3. How do you think social media undermines our ability to forge real friendships?
4. How can we keep social media from affecting real-life friendships?
5. How do you think the hypersexual nature of our culture undermines our ability to forge real friendships?
6. How can we counteract the hypersexual nature of our culture, and all its detrimental effects, in our personal lives?
7. How do you feel when someone remembers your name or important details about you?
8. What changes could your church put in place to ensure more people are noticed and remembered? What can you personally do?

---

renamed Saul on the road to Damascus, but "Saul" is called "Paul" in Acts 13:9 for the first time on the island of Cyprus, long after his conversion. The apostle Paul had dual names—a Jewish name (Saul) and a Roman name (Paul). As his missionary journeys took him from the land of his birth, he used the name Paul, perhaps to indicate his radical commitment to missionary work, becoming "all things to all people, that by all means I might save some" (1 Cor. 9:22).

9. Young adults expressed a desire for churches to be "caring but not creepy"—in other words, a balance between remembering them and not being overbearing. What can your church do to strike that balance? What about you personally?

10. Do you believe that belonging is a core desire of all humans? Why or why not?

CHALLENGE 1

How Can We Build Belonging?

> *He who loves his dream of a community more than
> the Christian community itself becomes a destroyer
> of the latter, even though his personal intentions
> may be ever so honest and earnest and sacrificial.*
> —Dietrich Bonhoeffer, *Life Together*

The cold seeped into my bones as I timidly rapped on the window. Snow whirled around me, shrouding me in darkness. I was hungry, for food and companionship, but no one heard my knocks. Through the double-paned window, I could see people laughing, hugging, feasting, *belonging*, but no one noticed me, the girl in tattered rags standing just outside. How I wanted someone to see me, to invite me in out of the cold and into the warmth. This is how I imagined my relationship with the church when I was a child and a teen.

In "A Theory of Human Motivation," Abraham Maslow states that love and belonging (friendship, family, a sense of connection), follow physiological needs (food, shelter) and safety. Maslow notes, "If both the physiological and the safety needs are fairly well gratified, then there will emerge the love and affection and belongingness needs, and the whole cycle already described will repeat itself with this new center. Now the person will feel keenly, as never before, the absence of friends, or a sweetheart, or a wife, or children. He will hunger for affectionate relations with people in general, namely, for a place in his group, and he will strive with great intensity to achieve this goal. He will want to attain such a place more than anything else in the world and may even forget that once, when he was hungry, he sneered at love."[1]

As we explored in the last chapter, young adults long to belong, to be known, and our faith compels us to meet that desire, to give people a space at our table. True community begins with love for the other, the outsider.

BELONGING BEFORE BELIEVING

In an astonishing departure from culture and tradition, Jesus initiated conversation with a Samaritan woman while on his way from Judea to Galilee. Around one o'clock, in the heat of the day, Jesus, weary from his journey, stopped to sit by Jacob's well near a town called Sychar. Tradition and culture effectively barred Jews from communing with Samaritans, let alone a Samaritan woman with a dubious reputation. But Jesus spoke to her anyway, asking her for a drink of water. Incredulous, she replied, "How is it that you, a Jew, ask for a drink from me, a woman of Samaria?" (John 4:9).

---

1. A. H. Maslow, "A Theory of Human Motivation" *Psychological Review*, 50, no. 4 (1943): 380–81, doi.org/10.1037/h0054346.

During this conversation, Jesus revealed who he was, the Messiah, for the first time. By engaging with the Samaritan woman, knowing full well who she was and the poor choices she had made, Jesus showed her she belonged before she even believed.

In his book *The Celtic Way of Evangelism*, George G. Hunter compares two different methods of evangelism: the Roman way and the Celtic way. "The Roman model for reaching people (who are already 'civilized' enough) is this: (1) present the Christian message; (2) invite them to decide to believe in Christ and become Christians; and (3) if they decide positively, welcome them into the church and its fellowship."[2] Hunter argues this method "seems very logical to us because most American Christians are scripted by it!"[3] Though the tide seems to be changing in the twenty-first century, this was true for the bulk of the twentieth century.

In contrast to the Roman method of evangelism, the Celtic model for reaching people was "(1) establish community with people or bring them into the fellowship of your community of faith; (2) within fellowship, engage in conversation, ministry, prayer, and worship; and (3) in time, as they discover that they now believe, invite them to commit."[4]

Before pastors even began to innovate methods for reaching young adults, they confronted the question: How do you build belonging among a people who do not know anything beyond the basic stereotypes of the Christian faith—stereotypes that are pervasively negative?[5] The level of secularity among America's population is stratospheric. Although America was not founded as a "Christian" nation, the foundational ideas of liberty and equality were tightly bound

---

2. George G. Hunter III, *The Celtic Way of Evangelism: How Christianity Can Reach the West . . . Again*, 10th anniversary ed. (Nashville: Abingdon, 2010), 42.

3. Ibid., 43.

4. Ibid.

5. Pastors also had to confront the question of how to build belonging among a people who have good reasons to distrust due to past "church hurt." We will discuss this in depth in chapters 9 and 10.

with religion at the founding of the nation. As Alexis de Tocqueville notes in *Democracy in America*, "The Americans combine the notions of Christianity and of liberty so intimately in their minds that it is impossible to make them conceive the one without the other."[6]

As Western society has become increasingly secular and Christianity has lost its cultural prominence and authority, many churches have adopted an evangelistic approach closer in alignment with the Celtic model of evangelism. However, the Celtic way of reaching others relies heavily on the personality and nature of the welcoming community. Along the way, some (though not all) young adult groups lost their joie de vivre, perhaps because of multiple leadership turnovers or stagnation. One young adult visiting one of the churches in the Kaleo Project bluntly noted, "Why would I want to enter into community with these people? They are cliquish and stale."

Author, educator, and theologian Marva Dawn expresses a similar sentiment in her book *Truly the Community: Romans 12 and How to Be the Church*. She observes, "As I travel around the country to teach, I am deeply saddened by our failure to be what God designed the Church to be. People who have been Christians for a while are not very often characterized by the profound gladness that marked the earliest followers of Jesus and that frequently bubbles forth in present-day new believers."[7]

The churches Dawn witnessed that were most successful in attracting and engaging young adults were those that exuded deep gladness and joy. Joy and the other fruits of the spirit that Christians are to demonstrate are compelling balms for the aches of loneliness.

---

6. Alexis de Tocqueville, *Democracy in America*, vol. 1, trans. Henry Reeve (New York: D. Appleton and Company, 1899), 329, https://www.google.com/books/edition/Democracy_in _America/r-oJAAAAIAAJ?hl=en&gbpv=0 .

7. Marva Dawn, *Truly the Community: Romans 12 and How to Be the Church* (1992; repr., Grand Rapids, MI: Eerdmans, 1997), xi.

BUILDING BELONGING: FIVE CHALLENGES

Denver is one of the most isolated major cities in the continental United States, surrounded by the Great Plains to the east, the untamed wilderness of Wyoming to the north, the deserts of New Mexico to the south, and the Rocky Mountains to the west. Yet it remains one of the top cities for young adults looking to relocate. Why do they come? Although Denver has a strong local economy, young adults claim they come for the weather and the outdoor activities.

So it was not a surprise that Kaleo churches found the biggest draw for young adults to be outdoor events such as hiking, biking, mountain retreats, and camping. These activities provided a common point of interest through which the believing and unbelieving could build relationships with one another. Learning how to engage young adults and build community demands fortitude. For the Kaleo churches, building belonging came with a number of challenges, and with each setback, pastors would assess what worked and what did not and would create innovative approaches to engage young adults.

CHALLENGE 1: RELYING ON OLD METHODS OF EVANGELISM (BIG EVENTS)

First, at the beginning of the Kaleo Project, many pastors and other church leaders assumed the way to engage young adults was through activities or "big events." They were surprised to learn how much young adults simply want to be remembered and to be members of a meaningful community. As one pastor noted, "Since the beginning of the project, we've become more aware and have reiterated that community is really important—even more important than events."

Josh, another young adult pastor, expressed a similar sentiment: "We've done some low-key events in the past, like a Superbowl party or something like that . . . [and] got a decent turnout. The one thing I found with events is maybe we get people there for that event, but there's not a lot of draw for them to come back unless they're already committed or unless there's already a relationship there."

CHALLENGE 2: REMEMBERING NAMES AND NEW PEOPLE

Second, pastors of larger churches or churches that were growing rapidly found it difficult to remember and recognize each individual. One young adult leader noted, "We've had pastors that I don't think could walk into any ministry outside of their own generation and name a single person in the room." One lead pastor of a large, growing church challenges all of their leaders to habitually memorize names of newcomers, but this isn't possible for every church.

To address this difficulty, leaders in these contexts often emphasized the importance of plugging young adults into small groups, which were often led by other young adults. Other churches used technology such as push buttons and instant messaging to connect with new visitors during the week and personalize their greetings and invitations to young adult groups. One young adult noted about her leader, "So, like, Hayley is a part of everything that we do. Like, she always texts us, like, 'Hey, what do you want to do?' We'll meet there, like, at that time, and [she] is always asking about people that can come or is always texting back to people that say, 'Hey, sorry, can't make it.' She makes everyone feel like they're seen and it's not like, 'Oh, I don't even realize that Malin couldn't come.'"

CHALLENGE 3: EXPANDING HOSPITALITY PRACTICES

Third, pastors were challenged to help their congregations grow hospitality practices beyond the standard "greet your neighbor" call from the pulpit. Overall, young adults find this practice awkward and inauthentic. Instead, some pastors urged their congregations to demonstrate hospitality to others, especially newcomers, on Sunday mornings through conversation and curiosity. David, a young adult from a larger church, described how leaders at his church welcomed everyone: "They have people . . . their job is [to] look for people that are sitting by themselves or [are] on their phone. I volunteered with their pre-team for a few months, and it was my job. So they're very intentional with how they place their volunteers . . . and they'll have a coffee bar, they'll have cookies or something like that to welcome people in. They're very welcoming."

Most of the churches in the Kaleo Project invited young adults to the homes of older congregants for a weekly homemade meal and discussion. One multiethnic church hosted a weekly Sunday international breakfast before the service, inviting people to bring dishes from their home countries or states.

For every church in the project, however different those churches were demographically or denominally, the most successful events involved sharing a hot meal in someone's home. Perhaps this is because so many of the young adults we encountered were curious about Christianity but had experienced a great deal of "church hurt," thus making the decision to attend an event off campus easier.

In many cases, these meals were hosted by people in the congregation who wanted to invest in the lives of young adults. In return, young adults enjoyed making themselves useful, arriving early to help put the finishing touches on the meal or prepare the table. One young adult, Jacob, noted a few studies that reveal an upward trend in those who say they have "zero" close friends. "I think we do suffer from lack of community," Jacob said. "And not just people to be around, but people who love us and grow us, people who, when we share a meal, it's in the essence of what Christ did when he shared meals with the disciples, not just eating food together."

The advantage of shared meals in private homes—especially for larger churches—is the intimacy it provides. As one pastor shared, "It's one experience to be with a thousand people on Thursday night. It's another thing to sit at a table and have a meal and have conversations and know the speaker personally." Another pastor agreed, "One of the things we wanted to say, or tell people, is this is the place where we want to know your name. We want to know your name, know your story. We want to get to know you. We have a capacity to do that in the [home] environment."

CHALLENGE 4: BREAKING UP THE CLIQUES

Fourth, congregations struggled to identify and address cliques that had formed among long-term members. Whether it was because a group had been together a long time or because they did not know how to engage newcomers, when new people came into an established group, they often found it difficult to connect. Sarah, a young adult, explained, "I feel like cliques have been my biggest issue with church and feel like I cannot get into anything. There are cliques [everywhere], but I don't know how to stop the cliques. You know, I don't know how to get them to be like welcoming. When cliques form, you cannot connect very well."

Being embraced by congregations, not just church leaders, was important to young adults. As Michael, a young adult leader, noted, "A lot of young adults are looking to peers and others in the church for support and encouragement and just a sense of hope." One church in our study had a problem with cliques because the youth and young adults had all grown up together. Another church simply had not trained their young adults to interact with newcomers. Finally, in another church, the cliques had transferred from school to the church.

People form cliques as a way of connecting with people of similar views, but cliques also provide a sense of safety. However, it is critical that the entire body of believers make new people feel as though they belong. If the leader is the only one showing hospitality, it's easy to think, *Well, of course they're nice to me—it's their job. They wouldn't care about me if they didn't have to.*

CHALLENGE 5: USING CONSISTENT, RELIABLE MESSAGING

Fifth, pastors had to overcome inconsistent messaging regarding group meetings, locations, times, and other events. Many young adults expressed frustration that information on young adult groups was not mentioned during the Sunday service or made readily available on tables outside the sanctuary. Others described conflicting or out-of-date information on the website or social media platforms. Still others, especially newcomers, expressed how hard it was to simply find where the group was meeting because of lack of signage. Even a small thing like a lack of signage or confusing signage might make church involvement seem daunting to newcomers and new believers.

Finally, pastors learned (or relearned) the importance of demonstrating hospitality from the church website all the way through the front doors of the church. After selecting the participants from our pool of applicants, I traveled to the physical location of each church to get a sense of how a young adult might feel approaching the church for the first time. At some churches, I found it difficult to figure out where the service might be held or what door to go through. Other churches made it clear where to go through signage or outside canopies. Such small details make a difference to young adults for whom just going to a church event demands great courage and energy. Demonstrating hospitality makes the process easier for young adults.

STUDYING HOSPITALITY: LIGHTHOUSE CHURCH

Lighthouse Church in Denver, Colorado, was founded in 2015 by husband-and-wife team Josh and Brianne Shaw. Josh and Brianne were both young adults with a young family when they started

Lighthouse Church, and today the church continues to attract young adults, giving them opportunities to serve at all levels. When young adult members were asked what they loved most about Lighthouse, many mentioned how well leadership remembered them. Preston, age twenty-two, stated, "I've been to churches where, after service, the masses just kind of go to the exit, and then that's it, rather than people talking. No one knew my name. At Lighthouse, it was different. People actually knew my name and stopped to talk to me." Brianne, who serves as the pastor of assimilation, said, "We value names above most things." Even as they grow, the Lighthouse team makes an intentional effort to remember people's names, whether through technology or through conversation.

The larger the church or the more a church grows, the more difficult it can be for staff to keep track of who is who. However, even the larger churches in our study were able to help people feel known and welcomed by prioritizing hospitality and exercising focused efforts similar to those of Lighthouse.

BECOMING A HOSPITABLE CHURCH

In summary, here are a few pointers to assist leaders and congregations in this area:

1. Host casual, fun get-togethers that target the interests of young adults in your area. Young adults often feel more comfortable in these environments and find it easier to invite friends who are not members of the church.

2. Hold some church events off campus. One term we often heard throughout our study was "church hurt." Many young adults who identify as Nones or are not part of a church community have negative associations with churches. Holding Bible studies off campus enables people interested in faith and

the Bible to get to know more about Christianity and meet others without the anxiety of "going to church."

3. Enlist regular church members to invite young adults to weekly studies and meals at their homes. Every church in our study found that regular small groups in people's homes around a meal were the most successful in terms of engaging young adults.

4. Ensure that all staff is trained in hospitality. When researching the locales young adults frequent, I came across Breckenridge Brewery, a brewery and restaurant just south of the Denver Seminary campus. When I asked what made them so successful, one manager explained that all staff—even the chefs who never see a guest—are trained in hospitality. When all staff are trained in hospitality, it informs their work. For churches, this is true from maintenance staff to IT all the way to the senior pastor.

5. Make sure your church is user friendly, from the website to the church campus or small group location. When approaching the church campus, how easy is it to find the sanctuary? Is there a system to ensure that messaging is consistent and reliable for small groups?

6. Make a focused effort to remember new visitors, and teach the importance of this to the congregation regularly. This not only releases pressure on staff to remember everything but also provides the congregation an opportunity to serve.

After more than twenty years of working in ministry, I have never forgotten that girl rapping on the windows of a church community, begging for someone to see her. I was the girl who did not feel wanted and did not feel she belonged because she carried too much pain, too much baggage, too much messiness. I was the girl who carried too many questions in her heart. I have never forgotten because, even now, immersed as I am in the work of the church, I recognize her presence within me still, longing to belong.

I felt as though I was the exception. I was the only one who had no place to belong, no one to notice me or remember my name. But my research and the relationships I have built with young adults and other "misfits" have taught me that those feelings of isolation and alienation from the church are the rule, not the exception. All people long to belong.

We are designed for community, not anonymity. While the technological culture promotes loneliness and anonymity, the church can, in its best form, provide community. It is true that one can find community outside of church, such as through sports, similar hobbies, CrossFit, yoga, Alcoholics Anonymous, the local bar, and many other options. In its finest form, the local church provides a place to engage with others who believe as you do, who support your growing relationship with your Creator. Without this relationship, all community is incomplete. As Saint Augustine of Hippo notes in his *Confessions*, "You made with yourself as our goal, and our heart is restless until it rests in you."[8]

QUESTIONS FOR INDIVIDUAL AND SMALL GROUP REFLECTION

---

1. Have you ever experienced feeling like an outsider, unable to break into a specific community? How would you describe that emotion?
2. What about the circumstances made you feel like an outsider?
3. Have you ever experienced feeling welcomed into a community? If so, how was that experience different from feeling like an outsider?
4. In what ways do you think the Christian faith compels us to welcome others?

---

8. Augustine, *Confessions, trans. Sarah Ruden* (New York: The Modern Library, 2017), 3.

5. Do you personally agree more with the Roman method of evangelism (believing before belonging) or the Celtic way of evangelism (belonging before believing)? Why?
6. What events draw young adults in your area? How can you or your church utilize these interests to engage them?
7. How important is hospitality to you or your church?
8. In what ways do you think you or your church could improve in the area of hospitality?
9. How important to you is it that others at your church know your name or something about you?
10. Do you think it is the responsibility of the congregation to remember and welcome others? Why or why not?

SEVEN

QUESTION 2

Am I Broken beyond Repair?

Teach me . . . Reach me
I know I'm not a hopeless case.
—U2, "Beautiful Day"

Like Atlas from ancient Greek mythology, young adults today are cracking under the weight of the world they shoulder. To enter their world, over the course of five years, I marinated in the culture of young adults. I wanted to experience, as best I could, the world as they knew it. I read widely outside of my own interests, books like the Hunger Game trilogy, *Fifty Shades of Gray* (yes, I did, and yes, young adults do too), *You,* and countless others. These books perpetuate a dark view of the world young adults inhabit. *The Hunger Games* is reminiscent of the Roman Coliseum's torture and depicts privileged spectators watching and betting as teens kill each other in the game. *Fifty Shades of Gray* popularizes the sexual fringe movements of

BDSM (bondage, discipline, dominance, submission, and sadomasochism) and sexual bondage.

While pounding out the miles on my treadmill, I watched episodes of *Black Mirror*, *Game of Thrones*, and *Euphoria*. *Black Mirror* warns of what can happen if we misuse technology. Each episode is a poignant commentary. Characters struggle constantly with technology, expressing existential crises brought on by pervasive use of technology. They share sentiments including:

- "Show us something real and free and beautiful. You couldn't. It'll break us. We're too numb for it."
- "People want to be noticed. They don't like to be shut out. It makes them feel invisible."
- "Authenticity is in woefully short supply."
- "There's no cure for the internet; you would never go away."[1]

I watched documentaries like *The Social Dilemma*, *Dark Girls*, *The Hunting Ground*, and *Swiped: Hooking Up in the Digital Age*.

The Social Dilemma, too, exposes the dark side of social media conglomerates, especially for young audiences. Some of the most chilling comments include:

- "If you're not paying for the product, then you are the product."
- "We're training and conditioning a whole new generation of people that when we are uncomfortable or lonely or uncertain or afraid we have a digital pacifier for ourselves that is kind of atrophying our own ability to deal with that."
- "We've created a world in which online connection has become primary. Especially for younger generations. And yet, in that world, anytime two people connect, the only way it's financed

---

1. "Black Mirror Quotes That Make You Think," Daily Brightside, April 27, 2022, dailybrightside.com/black-mirror-quotes-that-make-you-think/.

is through a sneaky third person who's paying to manipulate those two people. So we've created an entire global generation of people who were raised within a context [where] the very meaning of communication, the very meaning of culture, is manipulation."[2]

The voyage into the entertainment of young adults led me into a void, an empty place with no substance to grasp on to. Popular entertainment today aimed at young adults is rife with nihilism. Gone are the days of television sitcoms where the conflict of the story is neatly resolved within thirty minutes. Today, the stories on television and in popular books leave things unresolved and attach little meaning to the events that take place. The ruthless candor of these stories attracts young adults because that is how they respond to the world. As one young adult bluntly told me, "Since it is impossible to care about everything, I don't care about anything." Nihilism can be traced throughout millennia and is even addressed in Ecclesiastes. "Meaningless! Meaningless!" Qoheleth says, "Utterly meaningless! Everything is meaningless" (1:2 NIV).

There is a reason the apostle Paul urged the Philippians, "Finally, brothers, whatever is true, whatever is honorable, whatever is just, whatever is pure, whatever is lovely, whatever is commendable, if there is any excellence, if there is anything worthy of praise, think about these things" (Phil. 4:8). Even Nietzsche, often noted as the father of nihilism, wrote, "He who fights with monsters should be careful lest he thereby become a monster. And if thou gaze long into an abyss, the abyss will also gaze into thee."[3]

This interminable void authors many of the mental health issues

<hr/>

2. Emily White, "Six Chilling Quotes from 'The Social Dilemma,'" *Utah Statesman*, November 23, 2020, usustatesman.com/six-chilling-quotes-from-the-social-dilemma/.

3. Fredrich Nietzsche, *Beyond Good and Evil*, trans. Helen Zimmern (New York: Macmillan, 1907). 97, www.google.com/books/edition/Beyond_Good_and_Evil/yas 8AA AAYAAJ?hl=en&gbpv=0 .

plaguing young adults and their sense of being broken beyond repair. It is the nihilistic narrative in the stories proliferating throughout the entertainment industry that the church must answer with the hope of the gospel.

THE DARK IN WHICH WE HIDE

"You're not a beautiful and unique snowflake," reminds Tyler Durden, the imaginary alter ego of the Narrator in the 1999 film *Fight Club*. "You're the same decaying organic matter as everything else. We're all part of the same compost heap."[4] By 2016, *snowflake* was the *Collins English Dictionary* word of the year, meaning, "The young adults of the 2010s, viewed as being less resilient and more prone to taking offense than previous generations."[5] As Mila, a young adult interviewed for our study, said, "The narrative is, you know, millennials, Generation Z are snowflakes. They're sensitive, and they need safe spaces, or whatever." This reputation is the first reason young adults have suppressed issues with mental health. "Being called a 'snowflake' is damaging to mental health, young people say. Figures show that the majority of young people think the term is unfair—and even more think it could have a negative effect of its own."[6] In a study conducted by the insurance firm Aviva, researchers found that young adults are less likely to seek professional help because of the term *snowflake.*[7]

When I launched the Kaleo Project, I had certain ideas about who millennials and Gen Zs were. Perhaps, I speculated, a culture of

4. *Fight Club*, directed by David Fincher, starring Edward Norton and Brad Pitt (Los Angeles: Fox 2000 Pictures, 1999), DVD.

5. Sophie Gallagher, "What Does the Term Snowflake Mean and Why Is It Used?" *Independent*, October 6, 2020, www.independent.co.uk/life-style/snowflake-meaning-definition-gammon-piers-morgan-trump-b737499.html.

6. Olivia Rudgard, "Don't Call Us Snowflakes—It Damages Our Mental Health, Say Young People," *Telegraph*, December 6, 2017, www.telegraph.co.uk/news/2017/12/06/dont-call-us-snowflakes-damages-mental-health-say-young-people/.

7. Ibid.

"participation trophies" and helicopter parents had cleared obstacles out of their children's paths, leading to some character ramifications. In our first collaborative meeting with the Lilly Endowment and other participating organizations, one person mentioned they believed millennials and Gen Zs were the "prophets" God had sent to the church. I raised a skeptical eyebrow in the speaker's direction. But as I worked with this group of people over the years, I came to see the wisdom in this sentiment. What surprised me most was how deeply troubled many young adults are, how much pain they carry in their hearts, and how unwilling they are to be honest and open about their pain.

For years, younger millennials and Gen Zs were roundly criticized for their lack of resiliency. In 2015, research professor Peter Gray wrote that "emotional fragility has become a serious problem when it comes to grading."[8] He stated that some professors were "afraid to give low grades for poor performance, because of the subsequent emotional crises they would have to deal with in their offices." After a series of meetings, the counseling division concluded, "Failure and struggle need to be normalized. Students are very uncomfortable in not being right. They want to re-do papers to undo their earlier mistakes. We have to normalize being wrong and learning from one's errors."[9]

After more than a decade as a professor teaching both graduate and undergraduate courses in colleges and seminaries across the country, I must admit that I came to those same conclusions about the apparent lack of grit among younger generations. I was afraid to give lower grades, even when grading by a rubric. Many students complained about low grades, others agonized, and some demanded higher scores, as if their grades (and thus, my course) were a product they were purchasing.

But now I wonder: Are these emotional reactions evidence of lack

8. Peter Gray, "Declining Student Resilience: A Serious Problem for Colleges," *Psychology Today*, September 22, 2015, www.psychologytoday.com/us/blog/freedom-learn/201509 /declining-student-resilience-serious-problem-colleges.
9. Ibid.

of resilience, "the virtue that enables people to move through hardship and become better"?[10] Or are these reactions because of an inordinate, unprecedented number of challenges faced in a world of chaos and crisis? Since resilience, as a virtue, must be honed and sharpened, maybe the answer is somewhere in the middle. As Adam, age twenty-five, put it, "I feel like a lot of people perceive this generation to be so emotional and everything hurts their feelings. I think we're tougher than perceived because we're the first generation to grow up with social media from middle school [or] high school. And nobody has parented that, nobody else has gone through that, so we're kind of taking more bullying, we're taking more criticism. . . . It's not understood that we're dealing with a lot more than anybody else has as far as adolescence."

There might be something to Adam's point. In 2020, Deloitte, the multinational professional services network, published a study of 18,426 millennials and Gen Zs across forty-three countries that revealed "both generations remain resilient in the face of adversity and are determined to drive positive change in their communities and around the world."[11]

After the weight of being labeled "snowflakes," the second reason young adults are likely to withhold negative mental health issues is because of a perceived lack of understanding—or outright disregard—from older generations. Josie, age twenty-four, pointed out that mental health issues are "one of those things that older generations tend not to talk about as much. They weren't as open about it . . . and now our generation feels much more open about it, and it's become much like a problem." They are more honest about their emotions but often withhold them because they do not believe older adults will take their feelings seriously.

---

10. Eric Greitens, *Resilience: Hard-Won Wisdom for Living a Better Life* (New York: Houghton Mifflin Harcourt, 2015), 3.
11. "Deloitte Survey Reveals 'Resilient Generation': Millennials and Gen Zs Hard Hit By COVID-19 Pandemic, Yet View This Period as an Opportunity to Reset, Take Action," June 25, 2020, www2.deloitte.com/global/en/pages/about-deloitte/press-releases/deloitte -millennial-survey-reveals-resilient-generation.html.

To be fair, older generations faced (and still face) much more social stigma when it comes to admitting mental health issues. In 2010, the *American Journal of Geriatric Psychiatry* published a study that found "stigma associated with mental illness continues to be a significant barrier to help seeking, leading to negative attitudes about mental health treatment and deterring individuals who need services from seeking care," especially among minorities.[12]

Within both families and communities of faith, this divide can cause significant misunderstandings. For older generations, young adults may be perceived as weak or fragile, while younger adults may view older generations as rigid and dismissive. Peter, age twenty-one, said that when talking to older adults at church who asked him how he was, he thought, *I don't want to waste your time with all the things that are going on because I know you don't really care.* Mary, age twenty, agreed. "You don't feel like people genuinely care when they ask you how you're doing."

The third reason young adults do not share openly about mental health issues in the local church is because of the masks they wear. Younger millennials and Gen Zs find it difficult, if not impossible, to measure up to the standards of what they see on television and social media. "Our generation is a generation of comparison," one young woman declared. Another agreed, "Sometimes you don't have to post anything [on social media]. Sometimes it's just looking at other things and then looking at your life. And [it seems as though] what's posted on social media is the ideal of success." Ethan, age twenty-two, retorted, "Even though 95 percent of it is fake."

The natural dissatisfaction that sometimes comes in certain seasons of life is compounded when pressured to conform to an image, especially when that image has been curated and filtered. As Megan said, "Our standards of what success is, what happiness is, what beauty

---

12. Kyaien O. Conner et al., "Mental Health Treatment Seeking among Older Adults with Depression: The Impact of Stigma and Race," *American Journal of Geriatriac Psychiatry* 18, no. 6 (June 2010): doi.org/10.1097/JGP.0b013e3181cc0366.

is, what wealth is . . . all of those have been so filtered. You can go in and touch up and—"

"Filter," Jacob interjected. "I think we see so many people in our generation, and obviously even younger people as well, trying to create this fake image of themselves. Whereas when we're talking about constructive life skills—like being able to be open about things that bring awareness to problems that you have—that's certainly the opposite. [Social media] is all about hiding what . . . you're insecure about." For these young adults, the younger a person is, the deeper the depression will be because of their inexperience of life apart from social media. Jacob continued, "You'll see younger generations with even more problems with this because they've been having to deal with it for much longer."

FEAR

In 1980, German political scientist Elisabeth Noelle-Neumann published a prescient book titled *The Spiral of Silence: Public Opinion—Our Social Skin*, which hypothesized that most people are afraid of social isolation. To avoid social isolation, people observe other people's behavior and model their own behavior on those around them, frowning on behavior or opinions that are outside the norm. When loud expressions of opinion are expressed on one side, it silences other opinions and sets the spiral of silence in motion.[13]

While she could not have foreseen the power, pressure, or ubiquity of social media and the twenty-four-seven news cycle, her theories have grown more relevant with each passing year. Young adults today fear the power social media has in their lives. They fear, at best, round criticism for their views and, at worst, outright "cancellation." As Mike, age twenty-seven, put it, "In today's climate people are scared that if they speak their mind, then somebody's

---

13. "The 'Spiral of Silence' Theory," Elisabeth Noelle-Neumann (website), accessed October 7, 2021, noelle-neumann.de/scientific-work/spiral-of-silence/.

going to say something, and they think, 'I'm going to make them feel weird and they're not going to look at what I have to say.' So then they're like, 'Well, I guess I just won't [say anything], and I'll [keep it to myself].'"

Brian, age twenty-two, agreed, stating that there are opinions he never shares outside of church. "I feel more like the Christian voice is silenced: 'Don't say this, don't say that.' You say something the wrong way, and it seems like the world is against you when you just want to do what God has told you, to spread the gospel, tell them the good news. It's like, how do you do that when everywhere you go, no one wants to listen to you?"

Others are afraid that what they or others put out on social media might affect their future livelihoods, with many citing the case of Alexi McCammond, the twenty-seven-year-old who resigned from her post as the chief of *Teen Vogue* over tweets she posted when she was just seventeen.

SHAME

Over the course of our study, several young adult researchers observed how much shame young adults carry. They carry shame over previous actions and fear of judgment from churches, especially from older generations. As Taylor Miskel, a young adult researcher, wrote in her report for the Kaleo Project, "It is evident that vulnerability and love without shame is desperately wanted and needed for millennials to feel connected into a group or the church."

Young adults who were raised in conservative Christian environments expressed a great deal of shame surrounding sexuality. Amber, age twenty-three, admitted, "I think there's this idea [among Christian leaders] that if we just keep enough shame upon sexuality, that will scare anybody away from engaging in anything that we don't want them to engage. And then we don't maybe have to have the conversation if we just scare them enough. Purity is such a beautiful thing, but purity culture is just full of shame. And so then if you even find yourself in the midst of it, you're so shamed to talk about it or bring it forward. Sex, pornography, any of these issues, they've been hushed, [they have been] so blanketed and shamed that you just drown in it."

They crave leaders who will strive to see beyond the masks. "Christians do really good with masks," Mark said. "And so those leaders need to be strong to be able to pry that apart and be like, 'I know there's a great person in there. I'm going to get there.'" Tyler agreed. "We're not only craving those leaders that are willing to take a stand while they lead but [also those leaders] willing to take a stand in our own lives and really just be like, 'No, but are you okay? Are you really doing okay?' Being willing to step into that and really do digging because [young adults can be] kind of hard sometimes. You can't get past our shells sometimes."

One group described how awkward some gatherings can be in the beginning, with no one talking or connecting. "There's a lot of Thursdays or Saturday mornings where we'll meet, and one or two people say, 'This is going really poorly. I really don't know how I feel about this.' And then a few others decide to open up, and all of a sudden, ten people spill the beans about what's going on. And it's super refreshing. There's not many places we can do that."

Young adults do acknowledge that such vulnerability from leaders is difficult to balance. As one young adult noted, "It's kind of counterintuitive, right? We're all messed up, we're all broken, we all fall short, right? And the traditional church model is, 'I need you to get here.' Leaders put on this face where they're happy and joyous. And they think that people want that. And that if they put on that face, then people will come. But I think the opposite is actually true, right? [We want leaders who say], 'Hey, I really messed up, and I kind of broke my knuckle today because I was mad and punched something.' It's counterintuitive to say stuff like that, but that's a connecting point [for young adults]."

Angela, age twenty-six, pushed the point farther: "And when that attitude comes from the top, from the leaders, then the whole congregation follows suit, wearing a mask and pretending they're not suffering." Tamra, age twenty, agreed: "I wish that rather than [the church] being some club, it allowed us to share in our humility. And then I think good things just happen from that. Right? It's about meeting you where you're at, where you are."

THE DEMONS OF THE DARK

Young adults are haunted by a host of mental health issues, but the following are the "demons" they spoke of most frequently.

ANXIETY

One of the most frequently noted mental and emotional struggles was anxiety, particularly social anxiety. One young woman described her desire to connect with others but felt hindered by her own social anxiety. "I want the intimacy, but I'm afraid of the intimacy," she confessed. "I don't like to [go to church activities] because I get really high social anxiety, like really bad, and then I can't breathe. I would rather not go." Jayden, age twenty-three, chimed in, "There's an anxiety component to it. Just the contrast [of wanting] to have best friends, but I'm not sure who, where, or how, and if it's worth my time."

From his observations at several of the churches in our study, researcher Ryan Beerwinkle noted in one of our team meetings, "Young adults do not wrestle with angst or a desire to implement their will in the church. Rather, they wrestle with the anxiety of fitting into a church community. This is particularly evident in their approaches to the worship space." Similarly, one ministry leader pointed out the difference between Gen X angst and millennial anxiety. He hypothesized that while Gen X angst is rooted in the loneliness of their youth and their distrust of institutions, most anxiety experienced by young adults has to do with social anxiety and a desire to be known and to know others.

Beerwinkle continued, "Again and again, the theme of how young adults struggle with anxiety or how the overuse of technology prevents them from connecting relationally came to light."

DEPRESSION

Another concern mentioned by young adults was depression. On April 28, 2022, Forbes released information on a study in which 50 percent of young adults reported suffering from moderate or severe depressive symptoms, a marked difference from other age groups.[14] The young adults in our study that demonstrated depressive symptoms found it hard to engage with their peers in community, seek fulfilling jobs, and envision a more hopeful future.[15]

A HOPELESS CASE?

Even before the COVID-19 pandemic walled everyone away from one another, media headlines, television shows, movies, and academic research all pointed toward a looming mental health crisis, especially among young adults. In 2020, 21 percent of US adults (52.9 million people) experienced a mental illness.[16] The top three conditions

14. Deb Gordon, "50% of Young Adults Report Symptoms of Depression, New COVID-19 Survey Shows," *Forbes*, April 28, 2022, www.forbes.com/sites/debgordon/2022/04/28/50-of -young-adults-report-symptoms-of-depression-new-covid-19-survey-shows/?sh=4c672b415782.

15. *Sexual addiction, sexual assault, and eating disorders.* These issues were the proverbial elephants in the room. Women would quietly mention their struggle to overcome eating disorders and sexual assault. Men would talk about their addiction to pornography or their struggle not to objectify women. These conversations happened one-on-one, in private contexts, and there was a sense that a great many more people simply did not speak out.

16. "Mental Health By the Numbers," National Alliance on Mental Health, accessed June 2, 2021, www.nami.org/mhstats. NAMI breaks down these numbers further by the

afflicting this population were anxiety (approximately 48 million people), major depressive episodes (21 million people), and post-traumatic stress disorder (approximately 3.6 million people).[17] In 2020, suicide was the second most common form of death in those aged ten to fourteen and twenty-five to thirty-four, just after death by unintentional injury. Among all ages, there were twice as many suicides as there were homicides in 2020.[18]

Jason Murphy was twenty-four years old when he decided to end his life. Newly engaged, he was scheduled to start planning his wedding in mere weeks. Jason, a member of one of our participating churches, was a mechanical engineer who loved the outdoors—fly-fishing and exploring the vast Rocky Mountains. Both he and his fiancée were active volunteers at their local church, often helping with children and participating in their young adult group. His friends said he lived exuberantly and simply and loved fiercely. His suicide, like so many others, was sudden and unexpected. How could one who crackled with life decide to snuff it out? What brought him to that dark, desperate place?

Far too many young adults have dwelled in that dark place, the place where they feel like a hopeless cause, a lost case. Beyond hope. Beyond redemption. It feels like the end of the road. A prison with no way out. But with Christ, and the educated knowledge and care of the church, there is no hopeless cause or lost case. Anyone who is willing may be found.

following demographics: non-Hispanic Asian: 14.4 percent, non-Hispanic white: 22.2 percent, non-Hispanic black or African American: 17.3 percent, non-Hispanic American Indian or Alaska Native: 18.7 percent, non-Hispanic mixed/multiracial: 31.7 percent, non-Hispanic Native Hawaiian or other Pacific Islander: 16.6 percent, Hispanic or Latino: 18.0 percent, and lesbian, gay, or bisexual: 44.1 percent.

17. Ibid.

18. "Suicide," National Institute of Mental Health, accessed October 27, 2022, www.nimh.nih.gov/health/statistics/suicide.

QUESTIONS FOR INDIVIDUAL AND SMALL GROUP REFLECTION

1. Why do you think suicide is on the rise among young adults today?
2. What do you think of the term *snowflake*? If you are a young adult, have you been called this? How did that make you feel? If you are not a young adult, have you ever thought of young adults in this way? Why?
3. Do you think young adults are less resilient than previous generations? Why or why not?
4. How would you resolve the conflict posed by social anxiety—the desire for intimacy but the simultaneous anxiety about being in social situations?
5. Why do you think young adults are hesitant to speak about mental health issues with older generations?
6. If you are part of a faith community, have you experienced people wearing "masks" at church? If so, how does that make you feel? If not, what is different about your faith community?
7. Do you agree with researcher Taylor Miskel that "vulnerability and love without shame is desperately wanted and needed for millennials to feel connected into a group or the church"? Why or why not?
8. Do you agree that purity culture stokes shame? Why or why not?
9. Why do you think vulnerability is so important to young adults?
10. Do you think nihilism, the idea that life is meaningless, is on the rise? Why or why not?

EIGHT

CHALLENGE 2

How Do We Let the Light In?

> *There is a crack, a crack in everything*
> *That's how the light gets in.*
> —Leonard Cohen, "Anthem"

The best waitresses make great spies. They analyze body language, facial expressions, and casual asides between guests, and they quickly anticipate needs. They move swiftly, silently, imperceptibly serving their guests. And they listen.

One winter evening, one month after I returned to Christianity after a brief dalliance with atheism and agnosticism, I waited on a group of seminary students who had come into the restaurant where I worked for dinner after leading a youth group. I was intrigued by their descriptions of seminary, by what they were learning and how they were blessed by serving others, so I listened further. The two men admitted the high cost of seminary and how grateful they were that their parents helped them pay for their education. The two women agreed. Each one radiated with joy, unencumbered by the weight of poor life choices.

They stayed late into the night, laughing, joking, debating the finer points of theology and biblical studies. The longer they stayed, the farther I fell back into darkness. How different they were from me. They all hailed from intact homes, from wealthy, loving parents. They had never strayed too far from the path of the righteous. If they were the standard, what use could God have for me, a heathen, cracked and broken so many times over?

That night, I returned home bearing the full weight of my shame. Upon entering my apartment, I rifled through my closet for my "box" containing the last of the marijuana I'd been too afraid to throw away when I returned to the Christian faith. For so many years, marijuana had been my medicine, my way of coping with a broken home and a broken world and broken choices and the strain of putting myself through college. It removed me from myself. I grabbed the beautiful wooden box with the vertical pearl inlaid stripe and laid it to one side of the table in the center of my bedroom. On the other, I laid my Bible. My glance ping-ponged from one end of the table to the other. Two lives, two voices, warred inside my mind.

> **Voice 1:** It will be too painful to face all you've done. All that's been done to you. Better to numb yourself.
>
> **Voice 2:** Stay awake.
>
> **Voice 1:** I offer you oblivion.
>
> **Voice 2:** I offer you peace.
>
> **Voice 1:** You're not like them, Halee. You're too different. What is true of them will never be true of you. You've made your mistakes. You can't take them back. You carry them in your body.
>
> **Voice 2:** It was not one decision that led you here, to this place. It will not be one decision that leads you back and beyond from where you have fallen. And no, you will

never be like those seminary students. I have other plans
for you.

In the end, I put away the box and picked up the Bible, sensing both
spiritually and physically the solidity and weight of the Word of God.

VULNERABILITY AND AUTHENTICITY

The scene appears in three of the four gospels. Jesus saw Matthew,
also called Levi, sitting at the tax booth when Jesus called him. In
first-century Israel, Jewish tax collectors were despised by their own
people and considered traitors because they were hired by the Roman
government to collect taxes from the Jews. On top of working for the
Roman government, tax collectors often demanded more than the
prescribed tax to make their living.

When Jesus called Matthew as his follower, openly accepting him,
Matthew's joy was so great that he left everything and prepared for
Jesus a great feast (Luke 5:29). The guests of this feast included many
other tax collectors and people who the Pharisees described as "sinners." When Jesus heard the Pharisees grumbling at his disciples about
this, he said, "Those who are well have no need of a physician, but
those who are sick. I have not come to call the righteous but sinners
to repentance" (Luke 5:31–32).

For most young adults in our study, including the young adult
researchers embedded in these church communities, it was difficult,
if not impossible, to imagine themselves showing their weaknesses
and vulnerabilities at church. Everyone else at church seemed so "put
together," and prayer requests felt hollow compared to their own inner
needs. While some young adults silently contemplated suicide, others
voiced prayer requests such as "good term grades" or "patience manag-
ing a busy schedule." On the whole, young adults wanted an *authentic*
church experience.

QUESTIONS AND CHALLENGES

Over the years, we spoke a great deal about authenticity and what that term meant to young adults. We discovered that by *authentic*, they meant something close to the word *vulnerable*. We saw young adults who wanted someone to understand them, someone to model vulnerability and weakness. They wanted to be known and not judged. They wanted their church communities to come alongside them and say, "Hey, you may be struggling right now with different instabilities or different mental health struggles, or maybe you're struggling financially, or maybe you're just not sure about the future because the future that was promised to you hasn't materialized. Your questions and weaknesses are welcome here."

As Leilani, age twenty-five, said, "I just think a church like that gives you hope. Just knowing that we all [are] going through tough times. When someone else takes the time to really know what's going on in your life, you can lean on them and know, 'You know what? I can come out of this.'" Lucas, age twenty-nine, agreed. "It definitely takes a lot of weight off your plate. You always feel like you've got so much burden and so much overwhelming you, but when someone's there that has been through it who can help you, who understands and will talk to you, and you can talk to them . . . it's easier to just go through life, kick off a burden, all the stress."

The ubiquitous quote, "The church is not a museum for saints but a hospital for sinners" has been attributed to everyone from Saint Augustine to Abigail Van Buren. Churches aim and claim to be a place for the hurting and the lost, but that is not how young adults experienced most of the churches in our study. One young adult researcher described the dissonance between the tagline of one church, "Real, messy, new," and the experience of attending that church. From the building to the service, this researcher found nothing "real" or "messy." The building was impeccable, and the service was choreographed to perfection.

The researcher contrasted his experience at this church with a new church plant run exclusively by young adults. The building was old

102

and borrowed from a declining mainline church. "The church building reminded me of myself," he told me. "Imperfect. And it reminded me I don't have to be perfect to approach God."

CHURCHES THAT ARE HOSPITALS

When my fiancé, now my husband of more than twenty years, and I were trying to find a church home, I explained why one megachurch in our city did not seem like a good fit for us: "I don't want my church to feel so much like my sin." The fog lights and pretty people with perfect voices on a stage felt like the clubs I sometimes frequented in college. The feel-good sermons sounded like run-of-the-mill pep talks I heard from professors and popular, secular speakers. What was the point in attending church only to find what was so easily accessible in secular culture?

The megachurch movement has long been criticized for its approach to evangelization, but younger generations seem even less tolerant of such techniques. Why *are* only the "pretty people" onstage? Why are services so much like performances? Why attend church to listen to a sermon when the same message is available on a good podcast? The pastors and church leaders in our research sought to answer these questions by modifying their practices. What would it take to communicate that the hurting and the broken really were welcome in our churches—that indeed, our church community was *for them*? How could our churches be, in practice, hospitals for the broken?

First, church leaders discovered that young adults appreciate feeling needed. Contrary to what one might expect, at church they enjoy setting up for the service or event or cleaning up after. When attending small groups, they like to help with the meal and help the host clear up the dishes. For newcomers especially, these acts lessen their anxiety about being in an unfamiliar environment and help them forget their own insecurities. They give newcomers a purpose and help break the ice with other attendees. Allowing young adults to help is a simple way for churches to display their own vulnerability in "not having it altogether."

Second, although it seems superficial, details about meeting times and places should be as up to date as possible on websites and social media pages. This is extremely important to young adults. Many of my own researchers expressed frustration at last-minute changes to location, difficulty finding the appropriate location, and inaccurate times. Some of these changes were communicated within the existing community through group chats, but newcomers are not part of these group communications. As one of my young adult researchers wrote in a final report, "The best practices of this type of communication include a digital calendar that is on a website or Facebook page that is up to date, preferably [accessible] within one to two clicks of opening an app or getting to the home page of the website. With young adults struggling relationally, particularly with social anxiety, meeting at the time you say you're going to meet and having the atmosphere of the meeting reflect what is described online helps lower anxiety of individuals. Clear and accurate communication is a step toward building authenticity and trust."

When a young adult is spiritually and mentally desperate enough to seek out small groups in order to find a like-minded community, anything the church can do to make the process easier and less anxiety inducing is helpful.

Third, young adults benefited from small groups that focused on specific mental health issues. In recent years, many churches have referred those struggling with mental health issues to outside counselors or therapists. Unfortunately, this practice can reinforce the idea that church is for those who are not struggling, or to use the language of the Pharisees, church is for the "righteous" and not "the sinners." While there are people who certainly need the valuable professional help mental health clinicians provide, churches, too, can and ought to be places where people seek refuge from mental or spiritual anguish.

The mental health small groups offered by churches often had leaders who modeled their own difficulties and vulnerabilities, which positively affected how young adults experienced the groups. Will, age twenty-eight, said, "The best leaders are those who lead with their vulnerabilities. If somebody seems perfect, or if the perception is that they're perfect, that's not relatable because none of us are perfect. So if [a leader] comes off as perfect, it's like, 'I can't do what you do because I'm a human. I don't know what you are.'" Another girl added, "When I meet a leader or go to a new group, I'm thinking, *Can I trust you with my darkness? Can I trust you with . . . who I am?*"

Kyle Stanton, curate at Trinity Anglican Church, agreed, stating, "Authenticity is a buzzword, and so I think people get tired of it, but it's a buzzword for a reason. It speaks to something that people are craving. People crave integrity. And . . . integrity does not mean you don't have issues, doesn't mean you don't have faults, but integrity does mean you're honest about having those issues. And so young adults are craving integrity. They're craving people, leaders, who don't pretend to have it all figured out, who don't pretend that they are sinless and always make the right choices."

Fourth, church leaders found increasing value in addressing mental health issues from the pulpit. For newcomers, the weekly church service is the first point of entry to the church. It is only after attending a service that newcomers are typically connected with small groups. Young adults described how inspired they were when pastors spoke of their own struggles from the pulpit. Leah, age twenty-four, said, "If you hear a pastor or leader talk about how they struggled with alcoholism or depression and recovered from it, it's a really powerful testimony to somebody who is in the midst of that. They're letting you know that 'God can bring you out [of it] because he did it for me.'" Communicating the healing power of God in such a way from the pulpit teaches newcomers that their brokenness is acceptable in that church community.

Fifth, church leaders discovered that young adults place a high value on the experiences of their elders. They're searching for mentors who can help them navigate difficult life choices and circumstances. Ellie, age twenty-two, mentioned, "I think the older generations have serious hardships that they've gone through. I'd really love to learn the strategies they used to move past those hardships in their life and learn how to wait on God in those times of doubt and questioning."

One of the most successful events in our research was a series of panels featuring older generations speaking into specific issues that young adults face. Panels focused on grieving, finances, body image, and even dating. The facilitator would come prepared with a set of questions for the panel, and then the young adult audience was given time to pose their own questions. Young adults literally drove through blizzards to attend these panels and praised them.

Sixth, young adults longed for a mentor who would journey with them through difficult seasons of life, but mentors were hard to come by. Older Christians were hesitant to mentor for reasons including the busyness of their schedules, a lack of clarity about what "mentorship" entails, and a lack of confidence in their ability to help others. The churches that were most successful with establishing mentoring relationships followed these six steps:

1. They taught the whole congregation the importance of mentoring younger people in the faith.
2. They explained how older generations would be blessed by mentoring younger people.
3. They outlined the necessary characteristics of both mentors and mentees.
4. They clearly explained what mentoring was and was not.
5. They set boundaries for the mentoring relationships.
6. They organized a way for mentors and mentees to connect, either through an online platform or a physical message board.

Finally, church leaders discovered that young adults needed a place to "just be"—free of programming and activity. As David, one church leader, commented, "I think one of the causes for the uptick in anxiety and depression and some of the mental illnesses is . . . technology. I wouldn't say [the uptick is] 100 percent caused by [technology], but there's a link there to not being able to shut off or escape from the world, or always having to present an image, or just having issues follow you home. . . . It's constant. There's no time to just be. And plus, it takes away from real community, so we get fooled into thinking we have interaction and we don't. And so that, I think, leaves a hole within us to want and crave interaction but almost like we don't know how to get it."

Joanna, a twenty-six-year-old nurse, agreed. "I think the biggest thing that I've been aware of, as a Gen Z and a health practitioner, is how disconnected Gen Zs are. I feel like Gen Z is at risk of being the loneliest generation, having grown up without knowing any world without social media." Kelsey also agreed, stating, "People are much more willing to say hurtful stuff over text or over Snapchat or Facebook [or] Twitter because [it seems like] you're just talking to an avatar, not a real person. And that can lead to depression or suicide."

As one might expect, we found that the most restorative times for young adults were through regular social-media-free retreats with their peers and weekly gatherings at homes, around the dinner table, that provided opportunities for real connection.

CHURCH AS A HARBOR FOR BELIEVERS

Throughout the New Testament, Satan is referred to as the ἄρχων, the ruler, or the Θεός, the god of this world. In the book of Revelation, the apostle John reveals that ultimately, Satan will be defeated. Until then, it is the church's duty to serve as a hospital for sinners, for those coming out of the darkness, for those struggling deeply in a broken world. In a world hostile to the Christian faith, the church must also be a safe harbor for believers. It can be difficult to build a community comprised of people with diverse faith journeys, but with proper teaching and training, this type of community is possible for all congregations.

The light gets in when we remember people are not perfect.

The light gets in when we remember *we* are not perfect.

The light gets in when we remember we cannot offer God (nor anyone else) perfection.

The light gets in when we "ring the bells that still can ring,"[1] when we accept our own failures, our own weaknesses, and use them to reach others to whom we relate.

As of this writing, twenty-two years have passed since I picked up the Bible that evening, the day I chose to continue to live in the light. Although there are days the darkness still haunts me, what I experience today cannot be compared to the inky, terrifying darkness that once cloaked my entire being. I strive not to forget how it felt to live in great darkness so that I may remain empathetic to those who still dwell there and model the way out of that darkness. As Henri Nouwen states in *The Wounded Healer*, "The great illusion of leadership is to think that man can be led out of the desert by someone who has never been there."[2] God uses our lives, our stories, broken as they are, to reach the kind of people we once were.

This is how the light gets in.

---

1. "Anthem," Spotify, track 5 on Leonard Cohen, *The Future*, Sony Music Entertainment, 1992.

2. Henri Nouwen, *The Wounded Healer: Ministry in Contemporary Society* (1972; repr., New York: Doubleday, 1990), 72.

QUESTIONS FOR INDIVIDUAL AND SMALL GROUP REFLECTION

---

1. There are many ways to escape, ways we can check out of our lives—drugs, food, even Netflix. What are some of the ways you have tried to escape?
2. What is the core temptation of the desire to seek oblivion?
3. Have you ever dealt with shame about your past? How did you cope with it?
4. What do the Scriptures say about shame? Why can it be so hard to let go of shame?
5. How can Matthew's joy over Jesus' acceptance inform us about how to let go of shame?
6. What are some practical ways your church can make space for people to be vulnerable about their lives?
7. Where are there opportunities for young adults to be useful in your faith community?
8. Does it surprise you to know that young adults in our study craved the input of their elders? Why or why not?
9. Do you think mentors are hard to find? Why or why not?
10. How can leaders balance authenticity/vulnerability with modeling the way of Christ?

NINE

QUESTION 3

Where Do I Belong?

I have come home at last! This is my real country!
I belong here. This is the land I have been looking
for all my life, though I never knew it till now.
—C. S. Lewis, *The Last Battle*

Imari Johnson lived all her life in the same home in central Washington, DC, before moving across the country to Denver, Colorado, to pursue a master's degree in leadership at Denver Seminary. In addition to the challenges of moving cross-country for the first time, she arrived at a very different city from the one in which she had been raised. Denver was the furthest west she had ever ventured, and the big skies and isolation from other cities caused Imari a degree of anxiety. However, the most difficult aspect for her to adjust to was the lack of diversity in most churches and in the city as a whole. According to 2019 US Census Data, DC's population was 45.8 percent Black or African American while Denver's was only 11.1 percent Black or African American, with a large portion of those populations concentrated in downtown and east of the city.[1]

Imari, deeply committed to her faith, immediately sought a church home. One of the first churches she tried was Cripple Creek Baptist Church in the southern suburbs of Denver, despite the lack of diversity in that area. She said, "Initially, I was hesitant about attending a Sunday service at Cripple Creek. Mostly because [I had been] the only black person in a lot of settings in Colorado, and I did not want to experience that all over again at Cripple Creek. However, when I attended Cripple Creek, I was amazed by the experience I had. Yes, I was the only person of color, however, everyone was really nice, welcoming, and wanted to get to know me and my reason for visiting."

Surprisingly, what caused the most difficulty for Imari was not the lack of diversity but rather the way Cripple Creek Baptist Church divided their young adult group. "Cripple Creek does not meet exclusively with all young adults at one time; they break up into a variety of small groups based primarily on schedule," Imari said. "Young adults have the option [to choose] which group they would like to be involved in by signing up online. However, from experience, I am learning that most of the groups have people who already know one another."

When Imari finally selected a group that worked with her schedule, she arrived at the group only to find that it consisted of two married couples. Imari, single and a few years younger than the couples, persevered and tried to make the group work, but their life experiences were too different to make any meaningful connections. While Imari appreciated Cripple Creek's intergenerational approach to ministry, she still sought a place to make connections with people her own age.

Eventually, Imari found that elusive sense of belonging at Faith

---

1. United States Census Bureau, "Quick Facts: District of Columbia," www.census.gov /quickfacts/DC, accessed November 28, 2022.

Fellowship, which gathered young adults together as a group and often completed community projects together. Less than a week after visiting the church, the entire young adult group helped Imari move across town. Imari's story illustrates one of the most difficult barriers to young adults attending church: finding a place of belonging as young adults and integration into the whole church body.

MINISTRY TO AGES AND LIFE STAGES

Why do churches group people according to age? How did this practice begin? On any given Sunday, most evangelical churches provide Sunday school classes categorized according to age. From newborns to toddlers, through each corresponding grade in public school, parents can usually find classes uniquely tailored to their children's ages.

However, this was not always the case. Before the Arminian revivals of eighteenth-century England, the religious education of children remained the duty of parents.[2] According to Jeanne Halgren Kilde, the director for the Religious Studies Program at the University of Minnesota, parents "took their children to worship services, but in the meeting house children were relegated to the galleries, where a tithing monitor would keep an eye on them."[3] This practice was rooted in the Calvinist view that children were corrupt and uniquely vulnerable to sin. In the Plymouth Colony, parents were to make sure their children could read the Scriptures and understand "the main grounds and Principles of the Christian Religion."[4] According to church building plans from that time, classrooms for Sunday school were nonexistent.

---

2. Jeanne Halgren Kilde, *When Church Became Theater: The Transformation of Evangelical Architecture and Worship in Nineteenth-Century America* (New York: Oxford University Press, 2002), 171.

3. Ibid.

4. William Brigham, *The Compact with the Charter and Laws of the Colony of New Plymouth* (Boston, 1836), quoted in John Demos, *A Little Commonwealth: Family Life in Plymouth Colony* (New York: Oxford University Press, 1970), 104.

QUESTIONS AND CHALLENGES

Across the Atlantic, Robert Raikes, an Anglican and local business man of Gloucester, inspired by the teachings of George Whitefield, John Wesley, and Charles Wesley, "set about to evangelize children through education, focusing particularly on the children of the poor who lacked the literary skills needed for minimal conversance with the Bible."[5] Interested in improving the conditions of the working class, secular groups soon imitated the British Sunday school groups by providing similar education for youth.

Although church buildings in America "began to include Sunday school rooms in their building plans as early as the 1830s," the professionalization of Sunday school did not happen until the 1860s, when Sunday school became influenced by both the structure of secular education and the development of theories of child psychology.[6] In 1976 Rev. Dr. John Henry Westerhoff III published a book titled *Will Our Children Have Faith?* In it he outlines four stages of faith: experienced, affiliative, searching, and owning.[7] Just five years later, James Fowler set forth a theory of faith development based on six stages.[8]

---

5. Kilde, *When Church Became Theater*, 171.

6. Ibid., 175–76.

7. John H. Westerhoff III, *Will Our Children Have Faith?* (New York: Seabury Press, 1976), 89–99. In the experienced faith stage (preschool and early childhood), children grow in the faith through participation in the rituals and traditions of the church. At this stage, they imitate their parents and their surrounding community. In the affiliative stage (childhood and early adolescence), faith develops by belonging to a certain community. The third stage of faith, searching faith (late adolescence), is characterized by a questioning and testing of what has been taught. The final stage, owned faith (early adulthood), is a strong, personal faith.

8. James Fowler, *Stages of Faith: The Psychology of Human Development and the Quest for Meaning* (San Francisco: Harper and Row, 1981). Fowler's six stages of faith development are: (1) Intuitive-Projective faith, the stage of preschool children when fantasy and reality fuse together, (2) Mythic-Literal faith, the stage in which school-age children still believe the stories they learn from adults but also understand the world in more literal ways, (3) Synthetic-Conventional faith, generally reached in the teen years, in which the person adopts a belief system that attempts to encompass several social circles, (4) Individuative-Reflective faith, the stage in which young adults begin to critically examine their own beliefs, (5) Conjunctive faith, rarely reached before midlife, when people begin to accept the limits of applying logic to faith, and (5) Universalizing faith, a stage few people ever reach, but the few who do live out a life of service.

114

Born from these theories was the ubiquitous seeker-friendly based standard, where people are clustered according to age, life stage, or affinity. The benefit of these groups is no doubt the ability for some to find others in their specific life stage. The drawback is that these groups silo the church body. When I was a child attending a Southern Baptist church, the pastor would call the children up to him, offer a small sermon (and some candy), and then dismiss us from the service. If a baby happened to cry during service, the pastor would stop and ask the baby to be removed. Consequently, the church standard was to be siloed, and we rarely gathered as a group of all ages.

In most cases, churches outsource the curriculum for children's and youth group ministries from one of half a dozen children's ministry publishing houses that seek to blend child development with theology, including Group, Go, Grow, David C. Cook, Gospel Project, and Orange. After moving through children's ministry, youth group, and then college, church attendees "graduate" into the rest of the church body through a variety of means, such as regular Sunday service, young professional groups, or young married groups.

The organizational structure for Christian education according to age—from birth through college—corresponded well with American demographics until the 1990s, when the average age for a person to marry began to rise. In 1990, the average age for a woman to marry was twenty-four, just a few short years after one had presumably completed college. For men, the average age was twenty-six. According to the United States Census Bureau, as of 2021, the average age for both men and women to marry is now closer to thirty.[9] Now, in most churches, one finds a gap between college and married community groups.

---

9. United States Census Bureau, *Median Age at First Marriage: 1890 to Present*, figure MS–2, www.census.gov/content/dam/Census/library/visualizations/time-series/demo/families-and-households/ms-2.pdf.

CHANGES IN LIFE STAGES: MINDING THE GAP

The lack of groups for twenty-three- to twenty-nine-year-olds has left many feeling displaced—if not altogether unwelcome—at church. One young woman noted, "There's sort of a difference in reality between many of the members of the older generations and my current generation. In my parents' generation there was a seamless pipeline from cradle to grave. Their needs were addressed and met at every stage. Maybe that's not the reality, but it seems that way, at least to me. With my generation, there's a pipeline up until about college, and then you're just kind of spat out, and it's sort of like, 'Okay, now figure it out,' and [there are] not very many tools or resources to do that."

Amy, age twenty-five, agreed. "I went to a church where they had children's ministry, youth ministry, and then it just stopped. Not even a college ministry. They had small groups, but even in those groups I didn't feel like I belonged because I was too old or still single."

When searching for ideal community groups, young adults mentioned that they were primarily looking for three specific things: a place to be known, comprised of people in similar life stages, where they could grapple with deeper biblical and theological questions.

A PLACE TO BE KNOWN

Over the years of our study, the theme song to *Cheers*, a soundtrack from my childhood, played on a constant loop in my head because it was a sentiment I heard so often from young adults: "Sometimes you want to go where everybody knows your name."[10]

For some, being known meant being recognized and remembered,

---

10. Gary Portnoy and Judy Hart Angelo, "Where Everybody Knows Your Name: Theme From 'Cheers,'" Vocal Popular Sheet Music Collection (New York: Addax Music Co, 1982), score 5142.

as I mentioned in detail in chapter 4. However, it should be noted that this is not important for some young adults. Jaden said, "Well, part of me feels like maybe even if they forget your name, if they remember something and pick up the conversation from the last time they saw you, and they're still interested, they just forgot your name, maybe that's more forgivable." Adam agreed. "I guess it's like the personal engagement with you, and being open to being invested, and what keeps you busy during the week."

It is not surprising that those who displayed the strongest desire to be known were those who grew up in small churches and were now trying to attend churches in a larger metropolis, as Sarah did in chapter 5. This experience is not always shared by those who grew up in cities or megachurches. As Sienna noted, "In contrast, I grew up in a megachurch, and I've never been known at church, so that's not necessarily something I miss."

A PLACE WITH PEOPLE IN SIMILAR LIFE STAGES

When young adults described searching for a community of people in similar life stages, they often meant "single," "childless," or "career minded." When looking for other singles, young adults emphatically denied they wanted a "singles dating group." Rather, they wanted a place to connect meaningfully with other unmarried people. Jasmine commented, "When I say I'm looking for other people who are single—I'm not looking for a dating pool. I've been to churches with groups like that, and that's definitely not what I have in mind. Groups like that feel like there's an agenda—an agenda to get you married—from the get-go."

"Life as a young adult can be rather lonely," Rose added. "Especially as a single [person]. In today's economy, we work a lot of hours, and it doesn't leave a lot of time to socialize or get to know other people outside your workplace." The young adult group Rose hosts at her home provides her with an avenue for richer, deeper conversations—about life, work, or the Sunday sermon—with others in a similar life stage.

Regardless, single young adults do not want to be looked down upon by older generations. Susan said, "In church we learn about contentment, but I, unfortunately, don't feel very content when I'm talking to older Christians." She described a recent conversation with an older woman about her desire to go to Japan on a missionary trip, to which the woman responded, "Oh, you're not married yet? Oh, honey, God'll bring the right man along." Susan continued, "They're trying to be encouraging, to help [by saying] something positive, but I'd love someone to just say, 'It's so cool to hear what God's doing in your life right now.'"

The childless often felt as though they were missing a limb—some important part of their body. Greg, married to Jesse, stated, "You know, there's a lot of baggage in not having children. People think you have difficulty getting pregnant, and then they treat you like fine china, easily broken, or they think you are waiting to have kids or don't want kids, which they try to talk you out of." They say, "You don't know what a blessing you're missing by not having kids."

Career-minded women expressed their struggle to associate with women at church. Church programs seemed set up for families, as if the gospel applied only to them and not to single people pursuing a calling. Janet said, "I've tried for a long time to get connected with women at my church, but there are not a lot like me, with a high-profile job that demands a lot of time and dedication." She continued, "I would like more community with like-minded Christian professionals and would like to learn more about what the Bible says about work and calling."

In essence, whether single, childless, career minded, or all three, young adults long for their church to acknowledge that where they are in life is enough. They are not in limbo, waiting to reach another stage. Where they are, right now, is sufficient as long as they are walking with Christ.

A PLACE TO GRAPPLE WITH DEEPER BIBLICAL AND THEOLOGICAL QUESTIONS

The final trait young adults looked for in community groups was a place to go deeper into theology and the Bible. As Paul said, "After high school there's this sense of, 'Well, that was it. I'm off to the world, and everything I know is everything that I'm going to learn from church besides the Sunday service. There's no close group [in which] I can wrestle with the Word.'"

But young adults long for a community that can connect Scripture to the culture. "We're so 'in the world' the majority of our time, how do the truths of the Scripture shape how we live in the world?" Izzi asked. "And specifically, what do these truths mean for young adults?" Others echoed similar sentiments, expressing how spiritually beneficial it was to have a group that offered them wisdom on how to live faithfully in "a culture on fire."

Many mentioned the confusion they experienced while trying to discern truth in a world of "fake news" and "cancel culture." "You have so much information coming at you all the time," one person stated. "It's hard to know what's true and what's not. I mean, you can create deepfake videos of events that never even happened. But you can't question anything, or you might get canceled." Young adult groups provided not only a place to learn biblical truths on cultural matters but also a safe place to voice questions. Young adults are searching for a community that fully understands the reality they are living in, gives them a place "to commiserate over it," and then equips them with helpful, biblically based tools.

DISCONNECTION FROM THE CHURCH BODY

In recent years, some youth ministers have critiqued the efficacy of dividing church attendees into age groups. Timothy Paul Jones notes of his time serving youth, "What if, I wondered, this separation between students and adults—something that I was trained to see as a solution—has actually been part of the problem? What if God never intended youth ministry staff members to become the primary sustainers of students' spiritual lives? What if something is profoundly wrong with the entire way the church has structured ministries to youth and children? What if the reason so many ministers are bordering on burnout is because our ministry models are fundamentally flawed?"[11]

For Jones, the answer is to coordinate activities that connect age groups at church and return to the practice of assisting parents in their own efforts to disciple their children. Some researchers attribute the departure of young adults from the Christian faith to the practice of separating them from the greater church body. Without exposure to the greater church body, when they graduate from high school or college, they have completed "church" as they have always known it. As Kara Powell, executive director of the Fuller Youth Institute, mentioned on *The Stetzer ChurchLeaders Podcast*, "Of all the youth group participation variables we've seen, being involved in intergenerational worship and relationship was one of the variables most highly coordinated to young people's faith."[12]

Even though young adults expressed a desire for their own space, they do want to be connected in some way to the church, thus these observations are consistent with our research. Although young adults expressed appreciation for spaces where they could discuss how the Bible relates to them in their stage in life, many felt disconnected from the greater church body. Robert, age twenty-seven, confessed, "For a long time, I just wasn't interested in attending church at all.

---

11. Timothy Paul Jones, ed., *Perspectives on Family Ministry: 3 Views* (Nashville: B&H Academic, 2019), 7.

12. Brian Orme, "Our Most Popular Interview: Kara Powell and the #1 Reason Youth Leave the Church," ChurchLeaders (website), March 15, 2017, churchleaders.com /podcast/300757-popular-interview-kara-powell-1-reason-youth-leave-church.html.

It was like, well, the general Sunday service is for families and people past middle age and children, and the college-age people are ostensibly away at college. I felt like I had somehow fallen through the cracks, and no one cared. So if the church didn't care about me, then there was no reason to reciprocate [and] care about the church. At the very least, I figured, 'Until the circumstances of my life are different, I can't participate.'"

Many of the churches in our study were able to effectively integrate young adults into the greater church body, which we will discuss in the next chapter. However, many other churches were not as successful at integration, for a variety of different reasons.

First, some churches failed to consider young adults as potential members in the Sunday service, and thus the topics of the sermons and even examples fell short of any sort of relevance for young adults. One researcher on our team noted, "I had major questions about this church and service. Though there were some young adults present, most of the congregation was in their seventies or eighties, and during the sermon, the pastor offered a lot of health advice for older generations."

Second, some churches failed to let the congregation know—through online communications or announcements on Sunday morning—about the availability of young adult groups. In one interview with a millennial, another researcher noted, "She seemed interested in the opportunity to share her voice as a millennial into the young adult program at her church. She seemed very passionate about the disorganization and lack of action to meet the needs of young adults . . . [saying things] like, 'There was not anything for us' and there is 'a lack of communication' and 'tension.'"

Third, many churches struggled at the beginning of our study to find meaningful ways to develop intergenerational relationships. In one interview, a young man named Theo stated that the full extent of his interaction with any other generation was the two-minute "greeting time" during which he shook hands with others. "During the greeting time I shook hands with strangers, but it meant nothing in terms of community," he said. "It makes one feel welcome, but it feels like a check off the list."

SPACES TO BE KNOWN

The balance between having a space where they are known and finding ways to integrate into the larger church body is important to young adults. One side gives them an opportunity to be known, to get to know others in a similar life phase, and to apply Scripture and theological concepts to their context. The other connects them to something much bigger than themselves, to traditions that transcend time. Connecting with the larger church body also gives young adults a vision of life and faith beyond themselves.

The nature of qualitative research is exploratory—the whole point is discovery, and you never know what you might find. However, researchers never come to the task tabula rasa, with a blank slate. They have instincts, theories, or educated guesses at what they might find. When I first approached this study, I expected most young adults to display a cool indifference to the church, if not outright animosity. One of the biggest surprises for me was how much love for the church young adults expressed and how much they longed to belong. The criticisms they leveled at the church were born not of skepticism of the church but rather of a deep regard for it and its potential to change not only them but also the world in which they live.

QUESTIONS FOR INDIVIDUAL AND SMALL GROUP REFLECTION

---

1. What do you think of the practice of grouping people at church according to age? What are the benefits and drawbacks?

2. How important is it to you to feel known at the church you attend?

3. What are some ways you think churches can help young adults feel known?

4. Should churches strive to create groups for every life stage and every potential circumstance (e.g., singles, divorced, etc.)? Why or why not?

5. If churches do not have the staff or volunteers to create such groups, what are other ways they can help people feel included and welcome?

6. What do you think of Timothy Paul Jones's opinion that churches should focus on training parents to disciple their own children? What are the potential benefits and drawbacks?

7. Why do you think intergenerational worship seems to be highly correlated to the faith development of young adults?

8. Why do you think it is difficult for churches to balance providing space for young adults and integrating them into the greater church body?

9. Does your church have a "greet your neighbor" period? What do you think of this practice?

10. Why do you think young adults might feel left out simply because the pastor never references the existence of young adult groups?

TEN

CHALLENGE 3

How Can We Create a
Room of Their Own?

Listen to Mustn'ts, child, listen to the Don'ts. . . .
Then listen close to me.
Anything can happen, child, Anything can be.
—Shel Silverstein

here are no young adults in this neighborhood," the pastor said with shocking insouciance, spinning in his office chair and twiddling with his pen. "Besides, everyone knows millennials don't care about church anymore. It's just the way it is. I don't know whether or not it's worth my time to be involved in this project." His lips lifted in a half smile, his arms draped casually over the armrests of his office chair. As a researcher, I maintained an outward display of objectivity as I sat across from him, simply noting his indifference to the plight of young adults. Internally, I grieved. What hope would there be for young adults, indeed for the future of the church, if *pastors* had no hope?

Ideas have consequences. So claimed Richard Weaver in 1948 in his book of that very title. "Every man participating in a culture has three levels of conscious reflection: his specific ideas about things, his general beliefs or convictions, and his metaphysical dream of the world."[1] These ideas and beliefs then inform our actions, behaviors, and habits. This is true on the individual level as well as the collective societal level. Thus, the well from which we draw our ideas and beliefs is of great importance. Are we drawing them from the well of Scripture and Christian tradition, or are we drawing them from the fountain of information assaulting us via twenty-four-seven news and social media?

Over the course of our study, I noted that the greatest challenges for pastors emerged from their beliefs about the future of Christianity. Their beliefs were understandably informed by the articles and studies on the Nones. A quick Google search or Google alert reveals that new studies and articles on the Nones appear almost every day.

What happens in the mind and heart of a person who is told, daily, that their unsinkable ship, the Christian church, is doomed? These ideas had three consequences on the psyche of pastors and young adult leaders: acedia, fear of failure, and lack of support from senior leaders. These conditions were the primary challenges for pastors in building a space for young adults in their congregation.

ACEDIA

In T. S. Eliot's *Christianity and Culture*, he quotes the *Oxford English Dictionary* on the definition of the word *definition*: "the setting of

---

1. Richard M. Weaver, *Ideas Have Consequences* (1948; repr., Chicago: University of Chicago Press, 2013), 17.

bounds" (1483).[2] Without words, we cannot think, and tragically, some words have been lost, resigned to history. *Acedia* is one of those words, subsumed by the terms *laziness* and *sloth*. Without the word, we have lost the ability to diagnose this spiritual condition in ourselves and others.

The desert father Evagrius of Ponticus (345–399) was the first to write about acedia. Simply put, it means "a lack of care." Evagrius describes it as "the most oppressive of all the demons."[3] It is characterized by restlessness born of interior instability, an exaggerated concern for one's own health, an aversion to purposeful work, neglect of practicing spiritual disciplines,[4] and a general discouragement.[5] Of this general discouragement, Evagrius writes, "The soul . . . due to the thoughts of sloth and listlessness that have persisted in it, has become weak, has been brought low, and has dissipated in the miseries of its soul; whose strength has been consumed by its great fatigue; whose hope has nearly been destroyed by this demon's force; that has become mad and childish with passionate and doleful tears; and that has no relief from anywhere."[6]

Acedia is a deeper, darker, more powerful foe than what we know as "sloth" or laziness." It is born of something akin to depression and anxiety and burnout, leading to "great fatigue" and "loss of hope." Acedia is the place beyond the burnout. Acedia is the scorched earth of the soul, burning up anything useful within it. Acedia slyly whispers, "Is this worth it? All your zeal, all your passion, for such meager

---

2. T. S. Elliot, *Christianity and Culture* (1948; repr., New York: Harcourt Brace Jovanovich, 1967), 79.

3. Robert E. Sinkewicz, ed., *Evagrius of Ponticus: The Greek Ascetic Corpus*, Oxford Early Christian Studies (2003; repr., New York: Oxford University Press, 2006), 99.

4. Given his context of desert monasticism, Evagrius describes this as "neglect of the rule" (ibid., 40).

5. Jean-Charles Nault, *The Noonday Devil: Acedia, the Unnamed Evil of Our Times*, trans. Michael J. Miller (San Francisco: Ignatius Press, 2013).

6. Evagrius of Pontus, *Talking Back: Antirrhêtikos*, trans. David Brakke (Collegeville, MN: Liturgical Press, 2009), 142.

results? Did you make a mistake in discerning what to do with your life? Why not just give up? Why not just *sleep*?"

Evagrius called acedia "the noonday demon" because in the monastic context of the Egyptian desert, monks were most susceptible to acedia between the hours of 10:00 a.m. and 2:00 p.m., when the sun was at its zenith—the hottest part of the day. But acedia has no set hours, and it can eat away days, months, and years of our lives. Kathleen Norris notes, "Acedia, it seems, is not only the demon that lobs an assault at midday but also the bad thought that afflicts us in the middle of life, when it seems impossible to care about so many things that used to matter."[7]

Avicii, a Swedish musician and songwriter, composed a profound description of acedia in his song "Wake Me Up." "I tried carrying the weight of the world, but I only have two hands. . . . All this time I was finding myself, and I didn't know I was lost."[8] Avicii tragically died by suicide in 2018, five years after the release of "Wake Me Up."

The pastors in our study rarely spoke of their own spiritual and mental health, which is not surprising given their role in the faith community. Pastors are known to be reticent. However, we observed pastors exhibiting signs of acedia. The most tragic was the suicide of a pastor during the first year of our study. The pastor had built a strong reputation both with his congregation and those outside the church, but internally, he was struggling deeply. Though there are no direct statistics on the number of pastors who die by suicide, several recent high-profile cases have sparked a national conversation about mental health and pastors.[9]

---

7. Kathleen Norris, *Acedia and Me: A Marriage, Monks, and a Writer's Life* (New York: Riverhead Books, 2008), 200.

8. "Wake Me Up," Spotify, track 1 on Avicii, *True*, PRMD Music and Island Records, 2013.

9. "Pastors Have Congregational and, for Some, Personal Experience with Mental Illness," Lifeway Research, August 2, 2022, research.lifeway.com/2022/08/02/pastors-have-congregational-and-for-some-personal-experience-with-mental-illness/. In this study from Lifeway, about a quarter of pastors reported both diagnosed and undiagnosed mental illness.

More moderate displays of acedia in the pastors from our study included a persisting sense of discouragement about their ability to reach young adults and their calling as pastors in general. Some lacked direction and purpose. Some were burning out. Still others repeatedly missed important meetings and gatherings and canceled church events at the last minute.

All but a small handful began with the best of intentions. The pastors in our study were passionate about young adults, passionate about the church and its role in the world, passionate about Jesus Christ. Yet acedia afflicted many, especially during the pandemic.

Evagrius prescribes five remedies for acedia:

1. *Tears.* If acedia is "a lack of care," then the shedding of tears over our spiritual condition demonstrates that we do care. This is true on the individual level and the corporate level as members of the body of Christ. We can diagnose and grieve our personal spiritual condition and our spiritual condition as a united body of Christ.

2. *Prayer.* After the tearful recognition of our true spiritual condition, we should pray for our relationship with God, asking how we can be restored to spiritual health. We should pray over our calling and our work.

3. *Work.* The prescription here is an alternation between prayer and work. Pray. With prayerful purpose, set meaningful goals in your work. Pray. Work until you have completed your tasks. Avoid purposeless activity and distractions, like excessive researching on the internet (my own particular vice), scrolling social media, or any number of other things.

4. *Meditation on Death.* Western Civilization hides behind a facade of eternal youth and beauty. Our elderly, once the

---

Because of the nature of the pastor's role, one could reasonably assume the number who struggle with mental illness is much higher, with some pastors embarrassed to admit their struggle.

esteemed members of a community, are relegated to senior homes. We die behind closed doors. Research in neuroscience shows that when our brains receive information about our own deaths, they classify the information as unreliable.[10] To live well, we must remember we will die. With Moses we must pray, "Teach us to number our days that we may get a heart of wisdom" (Ps. 90:12).

5. *Perseverance.* The cunning nature of acedia means that it is difficult to discern and diagnose, and it undermines the prescription that will pull us out of its grasp. So we must persevere, working with purpose when we do not want to work, praying when we do not want to pray. When there is nothing left we can do, all we can do is endure. Not all pastors in our study succumbed to acedia, but many did. The ones who pulled through the experience of acedia, especially in the dark days of the pandemic, were those who had a strong community and were deeply supported by their church family.[11]

FEAR OF FAILURE OR INADEQUACY

Fear of failure afflicts about a third of the general population,[12] especially those who are perfectionistic, a trait that can appear in both low achievers and high achievers. Many pastors expressed a fear of failure. Some feared failure because they found it difficult to summon the resiliency to overcome past failures. Samuel, a fifty-nine-year-

---

10. Y. Dor-Ziderman, A. Lutz, and A. Goldstein, "Prediction-Based Neural Mechanisms for Shielding the Self from Existential Threat," *NeuroImage* 202 (November 2019): doi.org/10.1016/j.neuroimage.2019.116080.

11. Dom Jean-Charles Nault, *The Noonday Devil: Acedia, the Unnamed Evil of Our Times* (San Francisco: Ignatius, 2015).

12. Peg Moline, "We're Far More Afraid of Failure Than Ghosts: Here's How to Stare it Down," *Los Angeles Times*, October 31, 2015, www.latimes.com/health/la-he-scared-2015 1031-story.html.

old leader at a multicultural church, explained, "My church prior to this was two years of a massive, massive failure. I guess it's not just millennials—there seems to be, culturally, a growing deficit of resiliency. There's an inability to overcome hardship, or overcome difficulties, whether it's interpersonally or in your career." After his church failed, Samuel decided not to immediately return to full-time ministry work but continued to serve in a volunteer capacity at another church.

Some fear failure because they feel burdened by unrealistic expectations placed on them because of their race or gender. Catherine, age twenty-eight, graduated from seminary brimming with the hope of ministering to the poor, minorities, and domestic violence survivors through her local church. Shortly after graduation, she obtained a director's job at her local church working with these populations. She quickly grew discouraged under the stress of the high expectations placed on her as a young female in ministry. Catherine said, "There is not enough room for a woman in ministry to fail."

Elijah, an African American young adult leader, stated that he feels more pressure to succeed because he is a minority. "If you're a white male, you're judged as an individual. However, as a minority how you behave represents either positively or negatively on your group, right? So if you're given permission to lead [and] you succeed, well, wonderful. You now provided a positive example of how a minority can work hard and do well. If you fail, you have now shown them this is what happens when we give permission [to minority leaders]."

Another source of failure anxiety stemmed from pastors who were volunteers, with full-time jobs outside the church and families. Dave had a demanding career in finance but also volunteered as a leading pastor of his church with hours nearing full-time. At home, he had three children under five and a wife struggling with a debilitating illness. He loved his church and loved ministering to others but often felt like he was letting someone down. "I always joke that everybody's got their 100 percent of a pie, and only 100 percent," he said. "So at some point, it's either you're failing at church stuff, or you're failing at home stuff, or you're failing at work stuff in some senses. So that's been a balance thing and a learning thing."

Several pastors feared failure because of budgetary constraints. Kevin, age thirty-seven, set high expectations for himself as lead pastor but often felt boxed in by funding limitations. "My churches operate on a shoestring budget," he said, "and so you can kind of get in a rut doing things the way you've always done them." Even with funding from the project, it took Kevin and many other pastors a full year to break free of thinking constrained by their budgets and accept that they were free to fail.

Fear of failure stifles innovation. To adapt to cultural changes and create effective ministries, churches need to identify potential causes for fear of failure among their leaders. Church leaders need the support of both their congregations and other leaders as they strive to overcome their feelings of inadequacy. The freedom to fail unleashes creativity that enables leaders to analyze and overcome myriad problems, including financial difficulties. It frees the heart and mind to discover new avenues for evangelism and discipleship.

Even though pastors and other leaders often grew weary of failing and trying new things, with persistence, most remained consistently faithful in their love for young adults and their determination to make a meaningful difference in young adults' lives.

LACK OF SUPPORT FROM SENIOR LEADERS

One of the most important conditions of the grant and becoming part of the project was the willingness of senior leaders to invest in those who were leading young adult ministries. Yet, over the three-year term of the project, several churches floundered in their attempts to build a thriving young adult ministry because the leaders felt cut adrift from senior leadership.

The first church to leave the project did so because Eliot, the young adult leader hired to build a young adult ministry, did not get authority from senior leadership to make decisions. Eliot had to clear every decision through multiple levels of senior leadership, from the pastor to the elder board and then the congregation as a whole, which left him feeling as though his hands were tied when it came to innovating and making even small changes. Ultimately, Eliot quit his job at the church, leaving no one to continue their outreach to young adults.

At other churches, the leadership of the young adult ministry changed every few months because of a lack of support and direction from senior leadership. In these cases, senior leadership applied for the grant and the project, and once the grant was approved, they passed the leadership to volunteers with little training or direction. Under these changing conditions, the young adult groups failed to thrive. Lauren Schnackenberg, a researcher on our team, summarized in her final report, "Young adult leaders from [many of the] churches expressed the dynamic with senior leadership as . . . distant but supportive. The leaders feel supported in that their ideas are usually approved easily, they have been given freedom to do with the ministry what they want, and they have regular meetings or check-in times, but the senior leadership is not very involved personally in the ministry."

Will Freyschlag, the community life director at Parker Evangelical Presbyterian Church, believed that the support of senior leadership from the start of the project was key to their success: "I think one of the biggest pieces that has led to our longevity in the project has been senior leadership buy-in. I would say that if young adults' ministry is going to be tied to a church, you need to have the buy-in of your senior leadership. For sure, [you need a] team, even if it's just three or four people that can really take the reins with you. I think if any one person feels like they're running the whole deal themselves, they get burned out, and if there's not much accountability, the reach is not as far."

Throughout the project, Will achieved the fine balance of ensuring the young adult team had his support without making them feel as though they were micromanaged. At the beginning of each year, he met with the team over supper, and they outlined their plans and goals for the year. Throughout the year, he met with the team regularly and often showed up at events himself, as both he and his wife are young adults. In this way, the young adult team was led by young adults who were empowered by senior leadership to utilize their own giftedness.

A PLACE WHERE THEY WILL COME

At the beginning of our project, almost every church expressed doubts about whether young adults would come to their church. Several mentioned the high cost of living in the Denver metro area and how unlikely it was for someone in their twenties and early thirties to afford to live in such an area. Most had been trying for some time to attract young adults without any success. So, at the end of the project, it was incredibly moving when I conducted more than twenty focus groups at the end of the project in fall 2020 with more than two hundred young adults. Some of the young adult groups had grown so large that they were broken into smaller groups.

Despite the challenges, most of the churches in the project were successful in building thriving young adult ministries, even in areas where pastors doubted there were young adults living nearby. By the end of the Kaleo Project, the pastor at the beginning of this chapter had been let go because of moral issues (or immoral, as it were). When I conducted the final focus group meeting for this church, there were more than fifty young adults crowded around pizza, eager to talk to me about their lives, what they thought about church, and how glad they were the church had made a place for them.

QUESTIONS FOR INDIVIDUAL AND SMALL GROUP REFLECTION

1. What is the danger in pastors assuming a certain group of people is not in their church's neighborhood or not going to come to their church?
2. How is *acedia* different from "laziness"? How is it different from "sloth"?
3. How can a person who struggles with acedia also seem to be extremely busy?
4. Have you ever struggled with acedia? If so, did you manage to overcome it? How?
5. Why is it important to overcome a fear of failure?
6. How can the Scriptures help us overcome fear of failure?
7. Why do you think it is important that people who lead young adult groups have the support of senior leaders?
8. Why do you think a lack of this support emerged as such an issue in our research?
9. What are some ways that the congregation can ensure their pastors feel supported?
10. Do you think the tendency for churches to view Sunday service as a performance has a role in pastoral burnout? Why or why not?

ELEVEN

QUESTION 4

Can I Trust Christian Leaders?

*To be trusted is a greater
compliment than being loved.*
—George MacDonald

Jerusalem, AD 33. Just outside the gate of Damascus. A few yards
to the northeast loomed the skull hill, Golgotha, where Jesus had
been crucified only a few years prior. To the north was the garden
tomb, where Nicodemus and Joseph of Arimathea laid Jesus' body to
rest. The man on the ground was bloodied and broken by the stones
cast upon him. Stephen was not an original disciple of Jesus. He was
not an apostle. Stephen had been chosen by the disciples to oversee the
distribution of food to widows.

Yet he would not remain silent about the truth of God nor hide his
giftedness. He "performed great wonders and signs" (Acts 6:8 NIV),

but the Synagogue of the Freedmen were not happy with Stephen. They arrested him.

In his own defense, he recounted the story of the Israelites down through the centuries from Abraham to Moses. He said to the Sanhedrin, "You stiff-necked people, uncircumcised in heart and ears, you always resist the Holy Spirit. As your fathers did, so do you. Which of the prophets did your fathers not persecute? And they killed those who announced beforehand the coming of the Righteous One, whom you have now betrayed and murdered, you who received the law as delivered by angels and did not keep it" (Acts 7:51–53).

The words of Stephen as he faced certain death "cut to the heart" of the Sanhedrin, splitting them down the center. Overcome with envy and outrage, they stoned Stephen as he said, "Look . . . I see heaven open and the Son of Man standing at the right hand of God" (v. 56 NIV).

On that day, the persecution of those who followed Christ broke out, and the apostles scattered to the four winds to share the gospel. But no matter where they fled, they could not escape a similar fate. Jesus had warned them, "Beware of men, for they will deliver you over to courts and flog you in their synagogues, and you will be dragged before governors and kings for my sake, to bear witness before them and the Gentiles" (Matt. 10:17–18).

The martyrdom of the apostle James, son of Zebedee, one of the three in Jesus' inner circle (along with his brother John and Peter), is recorded in Acts 12:1–2: "About that time Herod the king laid violent hands on some who belonged to the church. He killed James the brother of John with the sword." Herod Agrippa ruled Judea in AD 41–44, and many scholars believe he killed James in an attempt to thwart the Christian movement.[1]

Although the deaths of the rest of the apostles are not recorded

---

1. Sean McDowell, *The Fate of the Apostles: Examining the Martyrdom Accounts of the Closest Followers of Jesus* (New York: Routledge, 2016), 190.

in the New Testament, church tradition and early historians provide insight on their fates. The early Christian writers Origen and Eusebius record that Andrew preached in Asia Minor and Scythia (modern-day Iran). Refusing to die as Jesus did, he was crucified on an X-shaped cross in November AD 60.

Flavius Josephus, a first-century historian, recorded the death of James the Just, the brother of Jesus, in AD 62. "[Albinus the Roman procurator] assembled the sanhedrim of judges, and brought before them the brother of Jesus, who was called Christ, whose name was James, and some others . . . and when he had formed an accusation against them as breakers of the law, he delivered them to be stoned."[2]

In John 21:18, Jesus told Peter his fate: "Truly, truly, I say to you, when you were young, you used to dress yourself and walk wherever you wanted, but when you are old, you will stretch out your hands, and another will dress you and carry you where you do not want to go."

After Jesus' resurrection and ascension, Peter preached and taught in Jerusalem (Acts 2:14–41); Judea, Galilee, and Samaria (9:31–21); and Caesarea (10:24–43). According to the early church fathers Clement, Ignatius, Irenaeus, Tertullian, and Eusebius, Peter ministered and was ultimately martyred in Rome during the reign of Nero sometime beween AD 64 and 67, hung upon a cross.[3]

The apostle Paul, like the apostle Peter, was martyred during the reign of Nero, sometime between AD 64 and 67, most likely by beheading.

Andrew, the brother of Peter, traveled to Scythia, in southern Russia, to preach the gospel before returning to Greece, where he was likely martyred sometime between AD 65 and 69.

---

2. Flavius Josephus, *Antiquities of the Jews*, trans. William Whiston (Auburn and Buffalo, NY: John E. Beardsley, 1895), www.perseus.tufts.edu/hopper/text?doc=Perseus%3Atext%3A1999.01.0146%3Abook%3D20%3Awhiston+chapter%3D9%3Awhiston+section%3D1.

3. Although this is not recorded definitively in the New Testament, it is alluded to in several passages (such as 1 Peter 5:13). There is an ancient account that Peter was crucified upside down, but this story comes from one source and therefore is not as reliable as the unified accounts from Clement, Ignatius, Irenaeus, Tertullian, and Eusebius.

According to Syrian Christian tradition, "doubting Thomas" doubted no more and embarked on a missionary journey to India where he was martyred in AD 72.

The apostle Philip preached in Hierapolis, in modern-day Turkey, and some historical accounts from the fourth and fifth century state that he was stoned and crucified there.

Bartholomew preached in Hierapolis, Lycaonia, Egypt, Armenia, and India. There are several differing accounts of his martyrdom, including drowning in Parthia, crucifixion with his head down in Armenia, and being flayed to death in India. Seth McDowell comments, "Of the variety of traditions regarding the fate of Bartholomew, no known traditions hold that he rejected his faith or died peacefully, but there is significant variety about how, where, and when he experienced martyrdom."[4]

James, son of Alphaeus, was martyred by stoning or crucifixion.

The apostle John suffered for his faith but was not martyred.

The fate of the other apostles, including Matthias, Simon the Zealot, Thaddeus, and Matthew are unknown, but all of them passionately preached the gospel until their deaths, even under great duress. While the fates of Jesus' followers are not proof of the resurrection, it cannot be disputed that their zeal and willingness to die for the sake of the gospel was one of the reasons Christianity spread so rapidly throughout the Roman Empire. People trusted their testimony. Their witness was deemed credible.

THE CRISIS OF CHRISTIAN LEADERSHIP

While it would not be hermeneutically or culturally responsible to fully compare the witness of early Christian leaders to the Christian leaders of today, young adults have a number of valid critiques that transcend

---

4. McDowell, *The Fate of the Apostles*, 215.

both time and culture. Both Christian young adults and young adult Nones raise concerns about the moral behavior of Christian leaders and a failure of effective checks and balances on how Christians are restored to leadership once a breach of character is revealed. Just a heads-up: in an effort to honor the anonymity promised to individuals in our study, the results of this section have been condensed, with less emphasis on quotations that might otherwise reveal individual identities as well as organizational identities.

Less than a month into the project, young adults in several churches mentioned the recent arrest of a former youth pastor in a nearby town. This former pastor, age thirty-five, was charged with an inappropriate sexual relationship with a seventeen-year-old girl in his youth group. In one focus group, young adults lamented how they wished the church would address moral failure among leaders, especially when it comes to sexuality. One young man said, "My heart hurts about the youth pastor that was arrested this week. Y'all heard about that? A longtime youth pastor was arrested for inappropriate sexual relationships with girls in the youth group." Another replied, "Yes, and that's not an isolated story; like school shootings, this is just this week's story."

That was February 2018. Just two months later, on April 10, 2018, Bill Hybels, founder and pastor of one of America's most prominent evangelical megachurches, resigned from his position following an exposé by the *Chicago Tribune* and an internal investigation alleging decades of sexual misconduct with staffers and women in the congregation. The *Chicago Tribune* investigated claims of "suggestive comments, extended hugs, an unwanted kiss and invitations to hotel rooms" which were "documented through interviews with current and former church members, elders and employees, as well as hundreds of emails and internal records."[5]

---

5. Manya Brachear Pashman and Jeff Coen, "After Years of Inquiries, Willow Creek Pastor Denies Misconduct Allegations," *Chicago Tribune*, March 23, 2018, www.chicagotribune .com/news/breaking/ct-met-willow-creek-pastor-20171220-story.html.

Nancy Ortberg, then a board member of the Willow Creek Association, lobbied for a "fair and thorough [internal] investigative process . . . that has high integrity which protects all parties in pursuit of what is true."[6] In an April 2 blog post that has since been removed, Nancy's husband, John Ortberg, former teaching pastor at Willow Creek and then senior pastor of the four-thousand-member church Menlo Park, stated, "I was approached over four years ago with disturbing information that I did not seek out. Along with others who received this information, I directed it to the elders of Willow Creek. The process that followed was, in my view, poorly designed and likely to expose any woman who came forward to grave risks."[7]

That same year, a volunteer and congregation member at Menlo Park privately revealed to John Ortberg a strong sexual attraction to children. Ortberg asked the volunteer if they had ever acted on those attractions, and when the volunteer denied any inappropriate conduct, Ortberg prayed with the volunteer, gave them a referral to counseling, and allowed them to continue to work with children at Menlo Park without bringing the matter to other leaders or to the church board. Church leaders did not discover this until the matter was brought to their attention by Ortberg's son Daniel M. Lavery. Although an investigation revealed no misconduct, Menlo Park accepted the resignation of John Ortberg in late July 2020 because "(1) Ortberg has broken the trust of many in the church, (2) it will be difficult to pursue the mission of the church while he remains a senior leader, and (3) he needs to prioritize reconciling with his family."[8]

In November 2020, Hillsong pastor Carl Lentz, who baptized

---

6. Ibid.

7. John Ortberg, quoted in Leonardo Blair, "Megachurch Pastor John Ortberg Calls Bill Hybels' Misconduct Investigation 'Poorly Designed,'" Christian Post, April 3, 2018, www .christianpost.com/news/megachurch-pastor-john-ortberg-calls-bill-hybels-misconduct -investigation-poorly-designed.html.

8. Jessica Lea, "John Ortberg Is Resigning as Pastor of Menlo Church," ChurchLeaders. com, July 30, 2020, churchleaders.com/news/379709-john-ortberg-resigning.html. While the identity of the volunteer and their relationship to the Ortbergs is important, I have elected not to discuss it here.

Justin Bieber in a bathtub at basketball player Tyson Chandler's home, was fired over an extramarital affair. In an email obtained by Religion News Service, Hillsong founding pastor Brian Houston attributed Lentz's dismissal to "leadership issues and breaches of trust, plus a recent revelation of moral failures."[9] The following April, another married Hillsong pastor, Darnell Barrett, resigned from his position as the creative director of Hillsong's Montclair, New Jersey, chapter over sexting allegations.[10] In January 2022, Hillsong founder Brian Houston resigned from all positions of leadership within Hillsong amid several scandals related to the use of Hillsong's tithes and an ongoing court case accusing Houston of hiding his late father's sexual abuse of children.[11]

Christian apologist and evangelical minister Ravi Zacharias was involved in ministry for forty years. In that time, he published more than thirty books on Christianity. After his death in May 2020, a four-month investigation found that Zacharias had hid "hundreds of pictures of women," abused massage therapists, and faced a rape allegation. As *Christianity Today* reported, Zacharias "leveraged his reputation as a world-famous Christian apologist to abuse massage therapists in the United States and abroad over more than a decade while the ministry led by his family members and loyal allies failed to hold him accountable."[12]

---

9. Roxanne Stone, "Celeb Pastor Carl Lentz, Ousted from Hillsong NYC, Confesses He Was 'Unfaithful' to His Wife," Religion News Service, November 4, 2020, religionnews.com /2020/11/04/carl-lentz-pastor-of-hillsong-east-coast-and-justin-bieber-terminated-for-moral -failure.

10. Hannah Frishberg, "Married Hillsong Pastor Resigns after Allegedly Sexting Church Volunteer," *New York Post*, April 28, 2021, nypost.com/2021/04/28/hillsong-pastor-resigns -after-allegedly-sexting-church-volunteer/.

11. Hannah Frishberg, "Hillsong Church Founder Brian Houston Resigns amid Scandal," *New York Post*, January 31, 2022, nypost.com/2022/01/31/hillsong-church-founder -brian-houston-resigns-amid-scandal/.

12. Daniel Silliman and Kate Shellnutt, "Ravi Zacharias Hid Hundreds of Pictures of Women, Abuse during Massages, and a Rape Allegation," *Christianity Today*, February 11, 2021, www.christianitytoday.com/news/2021/february/ravi-zacharias-rzim-investigation-sexual -abuse-sexting-rape.html.

Pastoral resignations in recent years are not all because of exhibiting or concealing sexually immoral behavior. Several leaders have also resigned because of issues related to spiritual abuse, pride, or anger. On October 14, 2014, Mark Driscoll resigned from Mars Hill Church because of heavy-handed leadership and abusive behavior.[13] Jason Meyer, who succeeded John Piper as the pastor of Bethlehem Baptist Church, resigned in July 2021 amid several allegations related to "toxic and abusive behavior of the church's leadership."[14]

These are just the cases we hear about. And they are the cases young adults in our groups spoke about. They command our attention because they command the news headlines, and even these are too numerous to name. We have no way of knowing how often this plays out in smaller congregations and smaller Christian organizations. Since a single case is one too many, we can safely presume it happens far more often than it should.

Many young adults also spoke to us in interviews about similar experiences of their own that never made the news, often because victims fail to report inappropriate or illegal behavior. Sexual abuse is one of the most dramatically underreported crimes, especially in contexts where the perpetrator holds a position of authority over the victim. Some young adults we spoke with never reported the incidents because they felt somehow responsible for making their pastor "fall into sin." Others simply wanted to move on from the experience—and away from the Christian faith altogether. A small but still troubling number of young adults admitted to romantic or sexual relationships with Christian leaders but viewed them as "consensual" rather than "abusive" despite the power dynamics inherent within the

---

13. Kate Shellnutt and Morgan Lee, "Mark Dricoll Resigns from Mars Hill," *Christianity Today*, October 15, 2014, www.christianitytoday.com/ct/2014/october-web-only/mark-driscoll-resigns-from-mars-hill.html.
14. Steve Warren, "'Painful and Confusing': Megachurch Pastor Who Succeeded John Piper Resigns," CBN News, July 21, 2021, www1.cbn.com/cbnnews/2021/july/painful-and-confusing-pastor-chosen-to-be-successor-to-john-piper-resigns-from-bethlehem-baptist-church.

pastor-congregant relationship. Speaking as a victim myself, reporting the crime felt like being raped all over again. Reporting such a crime demands great vulnerability, the kind of vulnerability stolen from us. The questions, the interrogations, feel like a violation.

What can we say about such horrors? I cannot speak for other victims, but I know that once I became a Christian, I left behind "worldly" friends, friends who made me laugh, who looked out for me, protected me, and never, a single time, took advantage of me. I cut them out of my life, shearing them away from my daily existence without so much as a goodbye. I needed, I thought I needed, to break free from their bad influence. I grasped hard on to Jesus and those I believed followed him. But one of those people raped me, and while he was raping me, the faces of the friends I had left behind floated before me, knowing they would have never deigned to do this to anyone. What more is there to say about such horrors—except that they should never happen? That we should be more careful about who we choose to put in power. That perhaps we should spend more time evaluating character rather than charisma.

CHURCH HURT

While the narrative of a leader's fall from grace usually centers on the leader, there is another aspect to these stories that is understated and far less understood: the impact on others. In recent years, the #metoo and #ChurchToo movements have launched a meaningful corrective to this by giving voice to the victims, but the ubiquity of the term *church hurt* used by young adults in our research indicates there are still many people who have been harmed by the immoral, predatory behavior of some Christian leaders.

Some who described struggling with church hurt were victims. There were women who had been groomed and abused by leaders of their youth group when they were in high school. Some had revealed the abuse to their parents or other leaders early on, while others had kept it a shameful secret for years. Some women were new Christians who were groomed by the leaders meant to be discipling them or providing spiritual direction. Some were young, married women who sought counseling from their pastor only to wind up in an extramarital affair. All of the women were in some way vulnerable to the abuser.

Of all the interviews we conducted, no men reported being the victim of sexually immoral behavior, but this does not mean there are no male victims. As hard as it is for women to disclose sexual abuse, it is even harder for men. Until 2012, the Federal Bureau of Investigation defined *rape* as "the carnal knowledge of a female, forcibly and against her will"—a gendered definition set in 1927. In 2012 that definition was expanded to "penetration, no matter how slight, of the vagina or anus with any body part or object, or oral penetration by a sex organ of another person, without the consent of the victim."[15]

The second group of people struggling with church hurt were the family members or friends of the victims. When victims do disclose abusive behavior, they usually go to trusted family or friends first. The first emotional response expressed by family and friends is usually shock at the dissonance between the public image of the leader and the experiences detailed by their loved ones. It is difficult to believe such a thing could happen. The shock is quickly followed by anger toward the leader and—if the incident is reported but not handled with grace, tact, and other appropriate measures—the anger is then directed at the church and Christianity as a whole. When such injustices are not addressed, it leads to disillusionment and disconnection from the church and Christianity. These people make up a sizable portion of the group we describe as the Nones.

The third group of people who have struggled with church hurt stemming from the immoral behavior of leaders are congregation

15. Susan B. Carbon, "An Updated Definition of Rape," United States Department of Justice Archives, January 6, 2012, www.justice.gov/archives/opa/blog/updated-definition-rape.

members or even Christians elsewhere who are disillusioned by the scandals they see reported in the news. Some of these people, too, come to describe themselves as Nones. If the church does not handle the incident well or fails to be transparent in order to save face or reputation, the church is viewed as complicit. Ultimately, the perceived complicity undermines the integrity of the leadership of the local church, the universal church, and the Christian faith.

EVANGELICAL PURITY CULTURE

The spiritual and psychological damage caused by the moral failure of Christian leaders is compounded by the shame many young adults experienced growing up in the evangelical purity subculture. The purity culture swept through evangelical churches in America and other countries, such as New Zealand, in the 1990s and the aughts.[16] In 1992, the Southern Baptist Sunday School Board launched the nondenominational True Love Waits campaign that urged teens and young adults to sign a pledge that read, "Believing that true love waits, I make a commitment to God, myself, my family, my friends, my future mate and my future children to be sexually abstinent from this day until the day I enter a biblical marriage relationship."[17]

In July 1994, 210,000 cards were exhibited on the National Mall in Washington, DC. The vow of abstinence was eventually accompanied by purity rings—silver rings worn by men and women as a symbol of their commitment to chastity.[18] In 1997, twenty-one-year-old Joshua

---

16. Although my discussion here is limited to the experiences detailed in my current research, while teaching in other countries I have met several women negatively affected by the purity culture movement.

17. Terri Lackey, "Internet becomes Symbol of Purity for 31,000 Teens Who 'Seized the Net,'" Baptist Press, February 15, 2001, www.baptistpress.com/resource-library/news /internet-becomes-symbol-of-purity-for-31000-teens-who-seized-the-net/.

18. Growing up as I did in the Southern Baptist Church, I, too, was an advocate of the purity culture. In 1992 at the age of thirteen, I lobbied for abstinence educational programs in

Harris published *I Kissed Dating Goodbye*, which sold more than 1.2 million copies worldwide. The book details Harris's disenchantment with contemporary dating and argues that "the attitudes and practices of our culture's dating relationships are unnecessary baggage that weighs us down."[19] Instead, he proposed a system of courtship and a commitment to abstinence before marriage.

While the campaign for abstinence was a well-intended response to the rise in sexual activity and sexually transmitted diseases among youth and was followed by a drop in sexual activity, it also resulted in negative consequences. In the area of sexuality, women were viewed as morally superior to men. Men were rightly encouraged to resist sexual temptation and lustful thoughts, but women were taught that they ought to help their brothers in Christ by dressing and acting modestly. The unspoken premise was that (1) women were responsible for men's sexual immorality, (2) women did not struggle with sexuality like men, and (3) your virginity defined your worth. This caused young women to experience shame about their own bodies and their own sexual desires. If women did have sexual activity before or outside of marriage, they believed themselves to be irreparable "damaged goods."

After interviewing several young adults who were new to church, our researcher Taylor Miskel wrote, "[Shame has] often resulted in two negative millennial reactions: either millennials can disengage completely or they lack appropriate boundaries in sharing life with others. If a millennial feels like a particular community is not authentic in their love, meaning the community is not supportive or welcoming to various cultures, that individual [is unlikely to] return or remain with the community."

Many young adults longed for the opportunity to vulnerably discuss the shame they carried from their conservative Christian

---

public schools while visiting with Democrat US House Representative Ralph Hall at his office on Capitol Hill.

19. Joshua Harris, *I Kissed Dating Goodbye* (Colorado Springs: Multnomah Press, 2003), 48.

backgrounds, and they wanted to be reminded that sin and shame did not define their worth or who they were as individuals. As one young adult told us, "The opposite of grace is shame."

The tragic irony of young adults' struggle with shame from purity culture is the profound contrast between the Christian leaders who advocated for sexual purity and their behavior. As detailed in the previous section, sex scandals have rocked the church in recent years. Some leaders of the purity culture now regret their part in it. In 2019, Joshua Harris divorced his wife and renounced both the Christian faith and his book *I Kissed Dating Goodbye*. In a 2019 interview with *Premier Christianity*, he admitted, "I think my writing really lacks nuance and balance, and for a lot of really impressionable young people it created a sense of real fear, and that had a negative impact on their view of relationships."[20] While promoting sexual purity to such an extent that it caused various levels of trauma to young Christians, Christian leaders were behaving the opposite.

THE REAL CRISIS OF CHRISTIAN LEADERSHIP

The innumerable scandals enveloping Christian leaders and our failure to faithfully respond to immoral behavior has wrought great harm. Every year since 1976, Gallup has conducted the Honesty and Ethics poll in which it asks respondents to rate "the honesty and ethics of 15 different occupational groups as very high, high, average, low or very low."[21] In just over a decade, from 2006 to 2020, the percentage

---

20. Sam Hailes, "Joshua Harris: Why I Regret Writing 'I Kissed Dating Goodbye,'" *Premier Christianity*, March 17, 2019, www.premierchristianity.com/home/joshua-harris-why -i-regret-writing-i-kissed-dating-goodbye/275.article.

21. Lydia Saad, "U.S. Ethics Ratings Rise for Medical Workers and Teachers," Gallup, December 22, 2020, news.gallup.com/poll/328136/ethics-ratings-rise-medical-workers-teachers .aspx.

of people who rated clergy highly for honesty and ethics fell from 58 percent to 39 percent.[22]

Some might dismiss these numbers as a sign of the end times. Some might blame Hollywood, the media, or left-wing politics for these numbers, and that might partially be true. But we cannot escape the fact that some of the blame is our own. We have not always held our leaders to the standards set by Christ. We have prioritized charisma over Christlikeness. We have not always demanded repentance before restoration. We have not used discernment or asked hard questions when disgraced leaders rise to their former positions or quickly replatform in another church or Christian organization.

This has damaged the spiritual lives of the victims, their friends and family, those surrounding the leader, and all who watch the fallout. It has damaged the way people view the church. It has damaged the reputation of all Christian leaders, for even the most faithful leaders cannot fully escape skepticism. It has damaged the reputation of Christ.

The crisis of Christian leadership is a crisis of character. The character of the early apostles stands in stark relief to the character of many Christian leaders today. The apostles were not perfect. They were common, ordinary men with flaws and imperfections. Peter was hotheaded and impetuous (John 18:10). The "Sons of Thunder," James and John, were, at times, selfishly ambitious (Mark 10:35–37). Thomas was pessimistic and doubtful (John 20:25). Judas was a traitor (Matt. 26:48–49). All abandoned Jesus to his fate on the cross (Mark 14:50).

In the wake of Jesus' crucifixion, Judas's remorse led him to suicidal despair. But beyond remorse is repentance, which includes remorse, an acknowledgment of wrong, an effort to make amends, and a "changed mind" resulting in changed behavior. Repentance is

---

22. Aaron Earls, "Americans' Trust of Pastors Hovers Near All-Time Low," Lifeway Research, January 22, 2021, https://research.lifeway.com/2021/01/22/americans-trust-of -pastors-hovers-near-all-time-low/.

a turning. "Produce fruit," John the Baptist warned the Pharisees, "in keeping with repentance" (Matt. 3:8 NIV). The remaining eleven disciples chose the path of repentance and demonstrated that through their actions on behalf of the kingdom of God, even unto death.

Now that the damage is done, what shall we do?

QUESTIONS FOR INDIVIDUAL AND SMALL GROUP REFLECTION

---

1. What made the disciples appear to be credible witnesses in the first century?
2. What makes the authors of the New Testament and the disciples they wrote about credible witnesses in the twenty-first century?
3. How do you think the recent scandals in both the Catholic and Protestant churches have harmed the credibility of Christians?
4. How does the credibility of Christian leaders affect the sharing of the gospel message?
5. What can churches do to restore the credibility of Christian leaders?
6. How can churches reach out and minister to the needs of those who struggle with "church hurt"?
7. How can churches strive to avoid hurting congregation members?
8. Do you think the purity culture caused too much shame for evangelical Christians? Why or why not?
9. How can we teach biblical sexual ethics without making the mistake of the purity culture?

TWELVE

CHALLENGE 4

How Do We Become Credible Witnesses?

Let us never fear robbers nor murderers.
They are dangers from without, petty dangers.
Let us fear ourselves. Prejudices are the real
robbers; vices are the real murderers. The great
dangers lie within ourselves. What matters it
what threatens our head or our purse! Let us
think only of that which threatens our soul.
—Victor Hugo, Les Misérables

B ishop Myriel was not always an upright man. The minor, but
pivotal, character in Victor Hugo's magnum opus *Les Misérables*
spent his youth "devoted to worldly pleasures."[1] But then came the
French Revolution, the Terror of 1793, the collapse of old French society, and the untimely death of his wife. He emerged from the ashes of

---

1. Victor Hugo, *Les Misérables* (New York: Penguin, 2013), 1.

these circumstances a changed man, devoted to the priesthood, and was appointed the bishop of Digne by Napoleon. He took up residence in the local hospital and gave the bishop's palace to twenty-six indigent hospital patients. Bishop Myriel donated 14,000 francs to various charities from his annual salary, allotting only 1,000 francs for his personal expenses. Donations poured like water through the bishop's hands straight to the hands of the needy. "Large sums of money passed through his hands," Hugo writes. "Nevertheless, nothing changed his way of life or added the slightest luxury to his simple life."[2] In all, Hugo devotes fifty-eight pages to describing the goodness and kindness of Bishop Myriel, "an upright man," before the good bishop meets the lead character, Jean Valjean.

When Jean Valjean is released from prison after nineteen years, every inn and lodging place turns him away because he is penniless and carries a yellow passport identifying him as a former prisoner and "dangerous man." Bishop Myriel offers Jean Valjean a seat by the fire, dinner, and a bed for the evening. Disbelieving, Jean Valjean says, "You are truly good. You don't despise me. You take me into your house. You light your candles for me, and I haven't hidden from you where I come from."[3] The bishop reaches out, touches his hand, and replies, "You didn't have to tell me who you are. This is not my house; it is Christ's. It does not ask any guest his name but whether he has an affliction."[4]

When Jean Valjean steals his silver in the night, the bishop tells the gendarme who arrests Valjean that the bishop gave the silver to Valjean, and he says Valjean forgot the candlesticks. When the gendarme departs, the bishop tells Valjean, "Do not forget, ever, that you have promised me to use this silver to become an honest man . . . my brother, you no longer belong to evil, but to good."[5]

---

2. Ibid., 8.
3. Ibid., 75.
4. Ibid., 75–76.
5. Ibid., 104.

THE SAVAGE SATIRE AND ASPIRATIONAL FIGURE

In a way, Victor Hugo was a None before Nones were a thing. The irony of Hugo's beautiful, inspired depiction of Bishop Myriel is that Hugo himself was anticlerical. For him, "faith [was] a question of feelings and love rather than ideas; it is impulse, emotion, giving, action, rather than theory or doctrine."[6] Hugo had heated discussions with his son Charles about the character, with Charles decrying priests as "enemies of democracy" and pleading with his father to craft the character "with a liberal, modern profession, like a doctor."[7] Victor replied, "I cannot put the future into the past. My novel takes place in 1815. For the rest, this Catholic priest, this pure and lofty figure of true priesthood, offers the most savage satire on the priesthood today."[8]

More than 150 years later, Bishop Myriel is an aspirational figure for many Christian leaders; for others, he offers the same satire. In our three-year work with congregations, one-fourth of the churches openly dealt with sexual scandals involving senior leaders. It is impossible to say if there were more, less visible indiscretions.

In one church, the senior pastor, whom I will call George, carried on an affair with a young, married mother of three children under five while his own wife was pregnant. The young mother had often posted on social media about her own unraveling marriage in the months leading up to the affair. When the affair was discovered, George was removed from his role at the church and immediately replaced by another long-serving pastor. For the most part, the affair was concealed from the congregation, and George and his family were honored with several farewell parties. George left the state to briefly serve in another ministry capacity but has since left professional ministry. At the time

---

6. Mario Vargas Llosa, *The Temptation of the Impossible: Victor Hugo and Les Misérables* (Princeton, NJ: Princeton University Press, 2007), 63.

7. Ibid., 64.

8. Ibid.

of this writing, George appears to be repentant and contrite, not only about the affair but also about his own selfish ambitions to become a megachurch pastor and how he abused his power.

In a second church, a charismatic young adult pastor, whom I will call Keaton, had an affair with a twenty-one-year-old who had recently started attending the church. Keaton was a young, married man with an infant son. The twenty-one-year-old was a new Christian, having accepted Christ after hearing the gospel presented to her by Keaton. The church had been struggling with other issues in leadership (not for any known abuse or immorality), and this affair caused the whole church to collapse. Eventually the church was integrated into another church. Young adults under this pastor were understandably adversely affected by the affair, and the young adult group attendance plummeted. To my dismay, I do not know what happened to the twenty-one-year-old brand-new Christian, how her life and her new faith were affected by this tragedy.

In a third church, a senior leader and founding pastor (whom I will call Tony) of a church plant was removed from his position of leadership after sexually immoral and domineering, threatening behavior was uncovered. At the beginning of the research project, a young woman approached and informed me Tony had a history of sexual immorality as well as predatory and vindictive behaviors. Since I had no evidence to act on this information, the church remained in the study. However, I did hold regular, transparent meetings with staff members who worked with this congregation about their feelings of safety and security for the duration of the project.

One year after the research had closed, another senior leader from that congregation contacted me to let me know that after multiple complaints of a similar nature (sexual immorality and vindictive, retaliatory behavior), Tony had been removed from his position of leadership. Even though he was working through a process of repentance, he would not be restored to leadership at that church. My deepest regret regarding this church concerns the young woman who fired up the initial warning flare to me in the beginning. This was not the only circumstance in which she bravely warned leaders about the immoral behavior of other leaders. To her, it may have appeared that all her warnings fell on deaf ears. She has since left the Christian faith, and I grieve the fact I did not let her know earlier that I had taken her words into account.

These are just some of the examples we saw in our research of sexual immorality and leadership misconduct. The #metoo and #ChurchToo movements have rightfully elevated the visibility and sensitivity to sexually immoral behavior, but there are other types of abuse as well that are not as easily defined or quantifiable, such as issues related to power. Two times each month, our research team gathered to discuss their ongoing observations and interviews in their respective churches, and often those meetings turned to discussions about the behavior they witnessed among church leaders. I met with many on the research team, all of them seminary students, one-on-one multiple times to discuss and work through their own despair at what they saw happening in the church. Some came in tears, frustrated by the staff dysfunction they saw in churches. One young woman said, "I don't know how long I can put up with these people!"

I smiled and said, "Do you know who you sound like?"

She peaked over the tissue and said, "Who?"

I said, "Jesus. 'How long shall I be with you? How long shall I put up with you?'" (Matt. 17:17 NASB). The important part for researchers coming to terms with their work was understanding the nature of church and the challenges the culture presents.

For these leaders, Bishop Myriel does indeed provide a "savage satire," illuminating the great difference between benevolent and malevolent leadership. It would not be fair to say that all or even most of the leaders we worked with during the project failed to live congruently with their beliefs and teachings. For them, I imagine Bishop Myriel is an aspirational figure, one they strive to emulate. However, the poor examples of leadership do cast a long shadow on the work and character of good leaders, damaging their credibility. One bad apple can indeed ruin the whole bunch. Or, as the apostle Paul teaches throughout his letters, we are all members of one body, and what happens to one affects all.

THE NEED FOR CREDIBLE WITNESSES

"You are my witnesses," declares the Lord,
"and my servant whom I have chosen,
that you may know and believe me
and understand that I am he.
Before me no god was formed,
nor shall there be any after me"

—Isaiah 43:10

The prophet Isaiah continues the declaration of God, saying:

"I, I am the Lord,
and besides me there is no savior.
I declared and saved and proclaimed,
when there was no strange god among you;
and you are my witnesses," declares the Lord,
"and I am God."

—Isaiah 43:11–12

The Hebrew word translated *witnesses* is עֵדָי (*e·dai*), which means "emphatically affirming" and is also translated in sections of the Old Testament as "evidence" (such as some translations of Ex. 22:13). In Psalms, Proverbs, Isaiah, and Revelation we read about the importance of a "faithful" or "truthful" witness. "A truthful witness saves lives, but one who breathes out lies is deceitful" (Prov. 14:25).

The book of John also emphasizes the concept of witnesses: the perfect witness of Jesus (1:7), the witness of the Holy Spirit (15:26), the witness of Jesus' works (10:25), the witness of Scripture (5:39), the witness of Jesus' disciples (15:27), and the witnesses of those who encountered Jesus (4:29; 9:25).

We cannot experience God through our five senses; one cannot see, hear, touch, taste, or smell God. God cannot be measured through scientific means. God is beyond logic, and therefore one cannot reason their way to God. This is why the faithful witness and testimony of Christians, especially Christian leaders, is so vital to evangelism. It is why the immoral behavior of Christian leaders has damaged innumerable personal relationships with God and the way the world views Christianity as a whole.

Like the people in the first century who saw and heard the testimony of the disciples, we need faithful, credible, believable witnesses to the gospel of the kingdom of God. We need witnesses who live not perfectly but faithfully, demonstrating what it means to be in a right relationship with God. We need witnesses whose lives demonstrate the transformational work of the Holy Spirit in our thoughts, attitudes, habits, and actions. We need witnesses whose lives are consistent with the doctrine they preach, and we need to hold those who fail to account. Only then will we be able to heal the damage done by hypocritical, harmful behavior and restore confidence in the church.

THE PATH TO BECOMING CREDIBLE WITNESSES

There are significant, important differences between criticism and critique. Criticism can often be mean-spirited, while critique is motivated by a concern for the good of another. Criticism is focused on finding fault, while any fair critique must be accompanied by sincere suggestions for improvement. To that end, we ought to consider two paths we must take to rehabilitate the reputation of Christian leadership in order to become credible witnesses both in our local churches and in the world at large.

ACCOUNTABILITY

First, we must commit to both personal accountability and organizational accountability. In the 1990s and early aughts, the concept of "accountability partners" took root in Christian circles. But because of a confluence of factors, the practice of having an accountability partner is not as common today, especially in regions outside the southern United States. Christians have long been blamed for being too judgmental, and we may have overcorrected to not voicing judgment at all. It is bad theology to be too judgmental, especially if you have not removed the plank from your own eye (Matt. 7:5), thus becoming a hypocrite. It is also bad theology not to judge at all. We are to judge—not those outside the church but those within it, especially leaders. In 1 Corinthians 5:12, the apostle Paul writes, "For what have I to do with judging outsiders? Is it not those inside the church whom you are to judge?"

Another reason for declining accountability is the confusion in our culture surrounding judgment. On one hand, we judge vociferously and publicly, often resulting in people being "canceled" over a single 280-character mistake. On the other hand, we soften otherwise strong statements with phrases like "my truth" or "your truth." Truth is not subjective, and it should not be scandalous to say so.

The final reason we may be less accountable to one another is because in many suburban churches, there is the sense that one ought to put their best face forward. A false face. This was true before the life-editing and filtering magic of Instagram, and it is definitely true now. If you are struggling, you might be accused of lacking faith. You might be rejected. You might not be met with compassion. It is hard to be real and authentic in a world so filled with fakery that we have forgotten what authenticity is.

Sadly, the same motive lies underneath both Instagram and organizational fakery: fakery is where the money and power are. Instagram influencers and Christian organizations are often in the same business of selling better lives, and that requires a bit to a lot of fakery. I realize that it might seem distasteful to say Christian organizations are "selling" better lives, but one of the reasons shallow leadership is such a problem is because the church has relied far too long on books and resources that appropriate business marketing tactics to the local church, and we have too often equated "what works" with making more money.

Accountability does not have to be painful. In fact, it should serve to alleviate pain. We can learn something from recovering alcoholics, who regularly move through the cleansing process of Steps Four and Five. Step Four involves conducting "a searching and fearless moral inventory of ourselves," and Step Five is admitting "to God, to ourselves, and to another human being the exact nature of our wrongs."[9] There is incredible freedom and joy in examining ourselves and knowing ourselves. Only once we know the ill may we find the cure. David knew this when he wrote:

> Search me, O God, and know my heart!
> Try me and know my thoughts!
> And see if there be any grievous way in me,
> and lead me in the way everlasting!
>
> —Psalm 139:23–24

And while I am grateful to Martin Luther that I am a Protestant, I have often longed for a place in the Protestant church similar to a confessional—a safe, sacred place in which I can regularly share my sins and struggles.

---

9. "The Twelve Steps," Alcoholics Anonymous, accessed October 28, 2022, https://www .aa.org/the-twelve-steps.

DISCLOSURE

The second path to becoming credible witnesses is to evaluate our disclosure methods. What do we tell congregation members when a pastor has fallen, whether from sexual immorality or abuses of power and authority? I do not have many answers here, but I hope to raise a conversation. At the very least, we should disclose as much as possible, but this will vary greatly because circumstances and organizations differ.

When it comes to sexual immorality, organizations should err on the side of more disclosure for the simple fact that the sexual immorality may have affected more than one person. For example, when the church in our study openly dealt with Keaton having an affair with a young adult, as mentioned earlier in this chapter, it caused a decline in the group, and many young adults were hurt in the process. But the group also provided a safe place for other young women to come forward with similar experiences. Such individuals knew their experiences would be heard and validated. Further, detailed and public disclosure makes it more difficult for a pastor or leader to leave one church or organization only to find another place to commit the same behavior.

Covering over a Christian leader's indiscretion may seem to make the most sense from both a spiritual and fiscal standpoint. Spiritually, leaders might think they are protecting the faith of other people in the organization. Fiscally, they may lose fewer donors and less money. But ultimately the potential harm that can befall others is too great a risk.

In 1999, long before #metoo and #ChurchToo, I wrestled with my decision to tell my senior pastor and the board of elders that the youth pastor not only was having affairs with two married women but also had sexually assaulted me. When I did so, he was immediately removed from his position and the parsonage where he lived, and I watched the fallout in the congregation. It was painful beyond words to behold, and I doubted I had done the right thing.

In the ensuing years, the question of how much damage my

actions brought became far less important than how much damage my inaction brought. That is the question that keeps me up at night. This pastor may have lost his job, been kicked out of seminary, and left the entire state of Texas, but he continued his education at another seminary and is a senior pastor today in another state. Had I pressed charges, that might not be the case. But I was just twenty-one years old, barely an adult, a new Christian, suffering from what I now know to be acute PTSD. I could not imagine surviving a police interrogation. So I let him go. I urge others not to make the same mistake, taking the easier way of concealment. We never know who that decision might harm.

THE POWER OF THE CREDIBLE WITNESS

Victor Hugo not only gave us an example of a credible Christian witness but also showed us the power of a credible witness. Myriel changes Jean Valjean's life, and the former criminal makes good on his promise to the bishop. The effect, however, is not immediate. Right after his interaction with Myriel, Valjean flees the town and, despite his newfound wealth, steals forty sous from a child. For twenty years, he nurtured his resentment and rage, taking refuge in it, until it filled his whole soul. The priest's pardon was "the hardest assault, the most formidable attack he had ever sustained," and "if he yielded, he would have to renounce the hatred which the acts of other men had for so long filled his soul."[10]

If he released the bitterness, the resentment, the rage, what of him would remain? "He had just passed through the decisive hour of his destiny . . . there was no longer a middle course for him . . . if he were not the best of men, he would be the worst."[11]

---

10. Hugo, *Les Misérables*, 109.
11. Ibid.

Jean Valjean becomes the best of men. He revolutionizes manufacturing and spends most of his wealth toward the benefit of the city. He accepts the position of mayor after turning it down once. He refuses the king's offer of knighthood. He rescues the orphan Cosette after caring for her dying mother. He is buried, per his request, in an unmarked grave. Victor Hugo's fictional world magnificently demonstrates that through the grace and benevolence of a single credible witness, God can bring forth an incredible amount of good.

QUESTIONS FOR INDIVIDUAL AND SMALL GROUP REFLECTION

1. Do you think Bishop Myriel is an aspirational figure that Christian leaders should aspire to? Why or why not?
2. How can the kind of grace demonstrated by Bishop Myriel turn a person's life around?
3. How does the character of Bishop Myriel compare to the leaders at your own church?
4. Why are credible witnesses important?
5. Have uncredible Christian witnesses or leaders caused you pain or confusion? In what way?
6. Are you able to honestly share your fears, failures, and mistakes with trusted people at your local church? Why or why not?
7. Do you agree with the statement, "Instagram influencers and Christian organizations are often in the same business of selling better lives, and that requires a bit to a lot of fakery"? Why or why not?
8. Why is accountability important?
9. How can it help leaders at your church?
10. Do you think it is important for churches to evaluate their disclosure methods, erring on the side of transparency? Why or why not?

THIRTEEN

QUESTION 5

Can I Ask Hard Questions?

We are closer to God when we are asking questions
than when we think we have the answers.
—Abraham Joshua Heschel

"Will you indeed sweep away the righteous with the wicked?"
Abraham asked the Lord when told of God's plans for Sodom
and Gomorrah (Gen. 18:23).

"Who am I that I should go to Pharaoh and bring the children
of Israel out of Egypt?" Moses asked the Lord when he was called to
advocate for his enslaved people (Ex. 3:11). And later, he asked, "O
Lord, why have you done evil to this people? Why did you ever send
me? For since I came to Pharaoh to speak in your name, he has done
evil to this people, and you have not delivered your people at all"
(Ex. 5:22–23).

"How long, O LORD? Will you forget me forever?" David asked (Ps. 13:1).

"How long, LORD, must I call for help, but you do not listen?" Habakkuk asked (Hab. 1:2 NIV).

"My Father, if it be possible, let this cup pass from me; nevertheless, not as I will, but as you will," Jesus asked in Gethsemane (Matt. 26:39).

Throughout the Scriptures, people whom God esteemed highly often question him—his motives, his actions, and his apparent inaction. Their questions are met with patience, the answers themselves blooming in their own time. God's people had to live into the answers. Occasionally, God responded to questions in sarcastic anger, as he did with Job:

> Who is this that darkens counsel by words without
>   knowledge?
> Dress for action like a man;
>   I will question you, and you make it known to me.
>
> Where were you when I laid the foundation of the earth?
>   Tell me, if you have understanding . . .
>
> . . . Have you comprehended the expanse of the earth?
>   Declare, if you know all this.
>
> Where is the way to the dwelling of light,
>   and where is the place of darkness,
> that you may take it to its territory
>   and that you may discern the paths to its home?
> You know, for you were born then,
>   and the number of your days is great!
>
> —Job 38:2–4, 18–21

(Confession: I adore this sarcastic side of God.)

But for the most part, the questions posed by God's chosen people tell us a few things about God:

1. He is not too small for our questions.
2. He is not confounded by our questions.
3. He does not feel threatened by our questions.
4. When asked in the right spirit, he is not offended by our questions.
5. When asked in the right spirit, he is not angered by our questions.

Why, then, have our churches become places where young adults do not feel the freedom to ask their questions? In chapter 2, I noted that all of the young atheists and agnostics who met for that first focus group had come from religious backgrounds. When I asked them how to raise my daughters so they would not leave the faith, every single person agreed, "Give them room and freedom to ask questions, and do not dismiss their questions with easy answers."

In our research, we found many young adults struggling with an inability to ask difficult questions in their churches. They felt stymied by a lack of precedent, a lack of venue to ask questions, and fear of judgment, among other things.

WHY YOUNG ADULTS AVOID ASKING HARD QUESTIONS

Many are the reasons people avoid asking sensitive or difficult questions. Many are the *places* people avoid asking sensitive or difficult questions. We avoid asking sensitive questions in the workplace because we do not want to appear incompetent or make unreasonable demands on a person's time. If you are a leader, you may feel burdened to have all the answers. We avoid asking questions in class out of shyness or fear of appearing slow-witted. We avoid asking our friends sensitive questions because we do not want to offend or appear intrusive. We avoid asking our spouses sensitive questions because we fear they might become defensive or because we are afraid of their answers.

There are five main reasons young adults are afraid to ask questions in a church context. First, there is fear of naming "topics that shall not be named." When I facilitated a panel of young adults in January 2020 at an innovation hub with local churches, just before the pandemic shut the world down, they expressed their desire for a place to discuss difficult issues. I let them expand on their views before I made the observation, "You all have just spent ten minutes speaking into your desire to ask difficult questions, but you have not named one example of what you mean by 'difficult issues.' We know you probably mean LGBTQ, gender identity, sexuality, theology, racism, and many others, but we do not know for sure. Why did you hold back from naming these issues you long to discuss?"

In short, they answered, "It is hard to name these things in front of a room full of pastors because we've never been given the opportunity to do so. We're not used to it."

Second, there is a lack of precedent for interactive, responsive forms of learning at church. Sermons are monologues, information imparted to an often passive audience, though some pastors and theologians believe this shouldn't be the case. In their book, *Preach: Theology Meets Practice*, Mark Dever and Greg Gilbert insist, "The preaching of the word of God is not a passive activity. It's not a mere meditation that stimulates the mind and goes no further. No, when we preach, we preach for change."[1] While small groups have become popular complements to the sermon, anywhere from 40 to

---

1. Mark Dever and Greg Gilbert, *Preach: Theology Meets Practice* (Nashville: B&H Books), 52.

60 percent of Sunday church attenders are not engaged in a small group.[2]

Over the years, hundreds of studies have shown that active learning—when students participate in their own learning versus listening to a lecture—increases "lecture attendance, engagement, and students' acquisition of expert attitudes toward the discipline."[3] Some studies indicate that active learning can increase a course grade by at least half a point.[4] But despite the evidence, the lecture often remains the preferred form of instruction in places of learning—and places of worship.

Third, young adults are hesitant to broach difficult subject matter because they believe baby boomers are very "black and white" in their thinking. As Amanda said, "I think the baby boomers, they saw everything black and white, and it was just like, 'Well, this is what our parents said, so it's true. And this is what we do. And we stick to it.' And it's like millennials . . . and the Gen Zs, we do not see black and white. We see every color of the rainbow, and we are questioning everything and trying to learn everything we can."

While young adults may feel Christian leaders and educators purport to teach "the truth" as right or wrong, with no room for debate or questions, it is an unfair assessment to say "baby boomers are black-and-white thinkers." Many in our society across generations have lost the art and concept of nuance. In a recent study from the Pew Research Foundation, rather than using social media as a platform for debate, 58 percent of US adults agreed that "calling people

---

2. Ministry Architects, "Church-Wide Norms," https://ministryarchitects.com/church-wide-norms/, accessed November 28, 2022.

3. Louis Deslauriers et al., "Measuring Actual Learning versus Feeling of Learning in Response to Being Actively Engaged in the Classroom," *Proceedings of the National Academy of Sciences* 116, no 39 (September 2019): doi.org/10.1073/pnas.1821936116.

4. Scott Freeman et al., "Active Learning Increases Student Performance in Science, Engineering, and Mathematics," *Psychological and Cognitive Sciences* 111, no. 23 (May 2014), doi.org/10.1073/pnas.1319030111.

out on social media" or "canceling" them is a way to punish people and hold them accountable.[5]

Fourth, and a testament to the diversity of opinion among young adults, some young adults do not address difficult issues to their churches because they do not want to force the church to take an official stand, thereby scaring off younger generations. Josh pointed out, "[Our leaders are] trying to build a congregation, not lose it. And [there is] such a fear with young people [that] if you say one wrong thing, [they're] out the door. They'll find somebody else that will believe what they do. That is a thing with our generation. We find people that believe the same things as us, and we move on. We're not as open to discussion and other viewpoints. We were tolerant, but now we're not necessarily going to change our beliefs for you."

And fifth, young adults do not bring up difficult issues because some are skeptical that older generations have the ability to address their questions. As one young woman said, "The generation before us didn't know how to talk about [difficult issues], and it was uncomfortable for them, so I think subconsciously and maybe unintentionally they were like, 'If we just keep enough shame upon this issue, that will scare anybody away from engaging in anything that we don't want them to engage.'" Amy agreed. "Yeah, like the whole purity culture . . . purity is such a beautiful thing, but purity culture is so full of shame. And so then if you even find yourself in the midst of it, you're so ashamed to even talk about it or bring it forward."

While young adults were skeptical their questions would be heard and meaningfully answered, they also believed their questions would be met with skepticism from older generations. Would other people question these young adults' faith? Would they dismiss their concerns? Would they still accept them as members of the community?

---

5. Emily Vogels et al., "Americans and 'Cancel Culture': Where Some See Calls for Accountability, Others See Censorship, Punishment," Pew Research Center, May 19, 2021, www.pewresearch.org/internet/2021/05/19/americans-and-cancel-culture-where-some-see -calls-for-accountability-others-see-censorship-punishment/.

QUESTION 5

WHEN QUESTIONS ARE NOT AIRED

The fact that young adults do not believe churches are safe places in which to pose their questions and air their doubts has serious and far-reaching consequences. First, and most important, when children grow up in church environments where serious questions are stifled and the issues that concern them are never openly and honestly addressed, they often leave the church as adults. In his book *Church Refugees*, Josh Packard notes that young adults dislike both the traditional, argumentative form of communication, in which two people state their position without the intention of swaying the other, and the dictatorial style of communication, where one person communicates and others just take it in. Rather, they have "a strong desire for authentic conversation."[6]

One young adult noted, "I would be dechurched today if I hadn't found my church, where we all sit around and talk . . . it's in relationships and conversations that I find God. It's not a real conversation if you're trying to convert me to your opinion. That's an argument. I'm not interested in arguing. That's not a real relationship either."[7] When they do not find those relationships in church, they join the Nones.

Second, when tough questions are discouraged—actively or passively—the church risks becoming irrelevant and out of touch. When people are not allowed to ask questions that haunt them, they sense that the church is not interested in their struggles or their lives in general. If the church is not interested in them as people, what, then, *is* the church interested in? Is it money? Power? Prestige? What is the point of church if not the spiritual formation and edification of people? What is the point in investing time and energy into an organization that is not invested in my spiritual formation and growth? Why bother?

---

6. Josh Packard and Ashleigh Hope, *Church Refugees: Sociologists Reveal Why People Are DONE With Church but Not Their Faith* (Loveland, CO: Group Publishing, 2015), 78.
7. Ibid. 77.

Again, as one young adult noted to me in a private conversation, "Why should I go to a sermon when I can just listen to a podcast?"

Third, when church does not allow people to ask difficult questions, they cut themselves off from conversations happening in the broader culture. Brian explained, "So then when we're surrounded by all these secular friends and all the world, it's like we don't ever have enough information that makes us fully understand something."

In other words, the secular world is teaching young adults what to think about certain issues. When churches do not address the conversations happening in culture, the secular world has the say at the end of the day. Brian continued, "I would rather be told exactly why [the church believes a certain way] and not like the way it sounds than just be like, 'It's my way or the highway, and that's it.'" Every person in the congregation is marinating is a secular culture that, in many ways, is contrary to the work and will of God, but this is especially true for young adults who spend so much time on social media and the internet.

Fourth, when young adults are not allowed to ask questions, they feel unseen, unheard, misunderstood, and unvalued in the larger congregation. One young woman longed for a church culture in which questions could be asked and answered, even if the answer was "I don't know." She said, "I would love to . . . have the church [that models] how to disagree on something because right now our culture is, 'If you don't agree with me and exactly how I think, you're a bigot, you're all these things. We cannot have any relationship.' And there's great power in being able to coexist in Christ and disagree and still be on the same team because we're all on the same side. And I would love to see the church model that, because our generation, particularly, is doing a terrible job of that."

To create a culture of inquiry, we have to hone our listening skills. The mark of an emotionally mature leader is the ability to listen to the questions posed by those who follow them and remain open and ready to answer those questions.

WHAT YOUNG ADULTS
WANT TO TALK ABOUT

I wanted to know what the "difficult issues" were that young adults wanted to talk about, so I asked them. As it turns out, their favorite question is also my favorite question: Why? One of the reasons I scored so poorly in some maths was because no one would teach me why. Why is math important? Why are letters and numbers put together? I resentfully struggled to find "x," wondering all the while what the point of it was. No one taught me that mathematics is the language of the universe. No one taught me that math is the most fundamental type of logic. If someone had taught me the why of math, perhaps I would have dug in and studied a little harder, and maybe the pieces would have fallen together for me easier.

Many young adults want to know the "why" behind the rules. Given the rise in the average age a person is when they get married, the topic of sex before marriage or living together before marriage came up quite a bit. "I think for me when I first was becoming a Christian," Liam said, "it was always like these are the rules, this is what you have to do, and there was never, like, a why behind the rules. I'd like to know the why behind these rules." Andrew agreed. "Talk about the whys for sure."

Another young man added, "I have a sister who's a teenager. She's seventeen. When I talk to her about sex before marriage, I really try to focus on why. She's raised in a Christian household. She's heard, 'Don't have sex before you're married.' She's heard that, but why?" Jacob jumped in: "There's a reason. Let's discuss the reasons and the whys behind these things and get more into God's viewpoint and his character and not just these broad black-and-white, yes-and-no things, but go more in depth."

Young adults also want to know the why behind church beliefs and traditions. Why can we trust the Bible as the authoritative Word of God? Why is it important to believe that Jesus was both fully God and fully man? Why do we need to believe in the Trinity? Why do we practice Communion? Why must we live in accordance with the Scriptures if Christ's death on the cross atoned for our sins? For many young adults, these are teachings they learned from very early in life. They accepted these things until they became adults and began evaluating what they believed and why they believed it.

Social issues are another topic young adults would like to openly discuss at church. What is our position on LGBTQ issues? Black Lives Matter? Racism? The flood of #metoo and #ChurchToo stories? They want to know not only the church's position on the topic but also the rationale behind it. Most important, they want to know how to love the people in their lives who may not live according to the principles set forth by the church. Amanda said she wanted to hear more about homosexuality and what to do "if one of your family members you love is that way? What if you yourself have struggles in that area? Do you have a space where you can talk about that? Do you feel comfortable with it?"

"I feel to ignore [the issue] and to look the other way, is so wrong," Billy stated. "I mean, I wouldn't say they necessarily have to back off from [their] hard stance, but they need to educate us on what the Bible says regarding [LGBTQ matters]." Derek chimed in, "They need to help us navigate what we should be knowing. Because I feel very well informed from politics, from the news, but there is no Christian response to balance what [the secular culture] is teaching us." Research from Springtide indicated that concern over LGBTQ issues was the largest gap between churches and young people. Seventy-one percent of young adults are concerned about this issue, but only 44 percent believe their churches care about the issue.[8]

Andrew agreed. "We know [we're supposed to] love everybody, and we know what sin is. But really, practically, in the culture, how do we engage with people who are in that community or who are

---

8. Ibid., 34.

advocates for that community. How do we engage with those people and maintain our Christianity and be loving?"

With astonishing wisdom, Andrew continued, "I think the extremes are easy. The whole bashing them. 'God hates you guys.' I think that's an easy path to take, but then also it's easy to just say, 'The Bible actually doesn't really have an issue with that.' I think those extremes are easy, but maintaining your faith in biblical truth while being loving . . . how do you do that practically?"

The extremes are easy. That's why nuance is a necessary creative art.

Young adults want to know how their faith should inform how they view racism and police brutality. In a focus group conducted in the fall of 2020, Lee commented, "Everything that's happened over the last six months has done a very good job of getting people to realize, 'Hey, there is still racism in our country.' However, it has not acknowledged that there is also a lot of racism toward Asian people in our country. We cannot just turn a blind eye to it."

Robin responded, "You know, we have to think about how to respond carefully because the church is the ultimate racism breaker. You look in Revelation, and it's people from all tribes and tongues. It's not just one tribe and tongue. . . . Jesus is the ultimate breaking-down barrier breaker."

Finally, many young adults expressed a desire for a fully articulated theology of the body, which included the role of women in the church, gender roles, sexuality, and mental health.

WHY WE WRESTLE WITH GOD

In her book *Searching for Sunday: Loving, Leaving, and Finding the Church*, Rachel Held Evans writes, "We don't want to choose between science and religion or between our intellectual integrity and our faith. Instead, we long for our churches to be safe places to doubt, to ask questions, and to tell the truth, even when it's uncomfortable."[9]

Like Jacob at the river Jabbok, we wrestle with God. It is hard, for example, to reconcile the cold realities of our world with the concept of a good God. How can the Holocaust and the existence of a good God be true? How can we give the whole of our lives to a cause or a dream, only to watch it slip away through our fingers? How can any type of love be wrong? How can parents abuse their children? How can a parent bury their child? How can people judge others by their race or gender?

How can it be so if God is good?

Why do dishonest people like Jacob, whom Frederich Buechner describes as "the shrewd and ambitious man who is strong on guts and weak on conscience, who knows very well what he wants and directs all his energies toward getting it" seem to do well in life? Buechner writes, "Jacob's kind of dishonesty, which is also apt to be your kind and mine . . . can take a man a long way in this world, and we are fools either to forget it or to pretend that it is not so."[10] Buechner notes, "This is not a very noble truth about life, but I think that it is a truth nonetheless, and as such it has to be faced, just as in their relentless wisdom the recorders of this ancient cycle of stories faced it."[11]

There are truths about the world that must be faced and questions that must be, if not answered, grappled with, just as Jacob grappled with God that night on the bank of the Jabbok. There are elephants to be addressed.

---

9. Rachel Held Evans, *Searching for Sunday: Loving, Leaving, and Finding the Church* (Santa Rosa, CA: Nelson Books), xiv.
10. Frederick Buechner, *Secrets in the Dark: A Life in Sermons* (New York: Harper SanFrancisco, 2007), 5.
11. Ibid.

QUESTIONS FOR INDIVIDUAL AND SMALL GROUP REFLECTION

1. What do the questions posed by people in the Scriptures teach you about them? About yourself? About God?
2. What questions keep you up at night?
3. In your personal faith journey, do you find it difficult to ask God certain questions? If so, which ones? If not, why not?
4. Do you struggle to *ask* sensitive or controversial questions in real-world settings (i.e., apart from online comments)? Why or why not?
5. Do you struggle to *address* sensitive or controversial questions in real-world settings (i.e., apart from online comments)? Why or why not?
6. What can you do to be more open to asking or addressing controversial topics?
7. What can your faith community do to be more open to asking or addressing controversial topics?
8. How often does your faith community provide forums or opportunities for the congregation to interact with leaders?
9. What are other difficult subjects or topics you think are important to address?
10. Why do you think churches are hesitant to facilitate spaces to address difficult issues?

FOURTEEN

CHALLENGE 5

How Should We Address the Elephants?

> *Byelinsky, like the Inquisitive Man in Krylov's*
> *fable, did not notice the elephant in the museum.*
> —Fyodor Dostoevsky, Demons

In 1814, the Russian fabulist Ivan Andreyevich Krylov published a page-long story titled "The Inquisitive Man." When a friend inquired about the man's day at the Museum of Natural History, the inquisitive man exclaimed, "I saw everything they have there, and examined it carefully. So much have I seen to astonish me, that if you will believe me, I am neither strong enough nor clever enough to give you a full description of it." He went on to describe the birds, beasts, dragonflies, butterflies, beetles, and gnats.

The friend replied, "But did you see the elephant?"

Surprised, the inquisitive man said, "Are you quite sure it's there? . . . Well, brother, you mustn't be too hard upon me; but to tell the truth, I didn't remark the elephant!"[1]

And this is the genesis of the well-known idiom "the elephant in the room." It captures the tendency we sometimes have to occupy ourselves with smaller, more manageable details in our organizations and lives because we cannot muster the strength or fortitude to face the elephant in the room. Either we do not know how to handle it, do not wish to handle it, or doubt our ability to handle it.

Like landmines on a battlefield, there are elephants everywhere—in Christian organizations, educational institutions, and particularly, our churches. In our churches, it is easier to tinker with worship style or the delivery of sermons or design elaborate church activities rather than address the elephants in our midst. The world has drastically changed in just a handful of decades, and we have largely failed to adapt in meaningful ways to these changes because, for various reasons, we are not addressing the elephants.

In our research, some churches were not ready to wrestle with the elephants. They continued the same tired practices they had for decades, hoping that the known approaches would help them with the new realities before them. Other churches were ready to wrestle and did so successfully, taking advantage of opportunities to host intergenerational panels on difficult topics or organize protests in their communities.

NOT READY TO WRESTLE

There were several reasons young adults said their churches were not spaces they felt comfortable bringing up difficult issues. First, some young adults felt that the cultural norm of the church was one of

---

1. Ivan Krylov, "The Inquisitive Man," in *Krilof and His Fables* (London: Strahan, 1871), 45, https://books.google.com/books?id=E0zvAgAAQBAJ&newbks=0&printsec=frontcover&pg=PA43&dq=Ivan+Andreevich+Krylov+the+inquisitive+man&hl=en&source=newbks_fb#v=onepage&q=Ivan%20Andreevich%20Krylov%20the%20inquisitive%20man&f=false.

avoidance. Sarah said, "It seems like our culture wants everything to be out in the open, and that's what we've grown up with. If there's something that might be controversial, it's better to talk about it than to ignore it or pretend that it's not an issue." And since that is the cultural response, she continued, "It'd be nice for the church to have that mentality of 'people outside of church are having these conversations, so shouldn't the church be involved in these conversations too?'" Kevin agreed. "Yeah, what's the church's perspective on these issues?" Another young woman disagreed somewhat, stating, "We need to hear about controversial subjects, and we need the church's position on them. Most people won't get into it, and if they do, they'll get into it and be nasty about it. You can't just have these kinds of conversations with most people because it's like, now we're picking sides as opposed to just sharing our viewpoints or whatever. That's just not a thing, generally speaking, these days that people can do as adults. So there's certain topics you avoid, not even just within the church but within society. You start this, and you're probably starting a war, or at least a fierce battle."

Peter shot back, "From Black Lives Matter to LGBTQ, everything. We shouldn't shy away from the issues, especially if we as the church are going to be a light, be a people group, in this city, in this nation, then we can't avoid these issues." Even though the young adults we spoke with didn't all agree where the line was in addressing these tough issues, most agreed that their churches had room to grow in this area.

Second, young adults noticed that some churches avoided addressing elephants because of fear. Heather said, "I think one of the biggest reasons we see division today is that the church body itself is too afraid to talk. Right? Because if we have a foundation in Christ together, but we disagree on these different things, that spreads from the church out into the public."

Peter agreed. "I just feel like they don't want to engage these issues [because they are] driven by fear. Like, 'We don't want to potentially create strife or just issues within the church by introducing these topics that are so binary, polarizing.'"

Josh commented, "A fear with young people is if you say one wrong thing, you're out the door. They'll find somebody else that will believe what they do. That is a thing with our generation—we find people that believe the same things as us, we move on. We're not as open. We were tolerant, but we're not necessarily going to change our beliefs for you. And so a church doesn't want to take a stance on our issues and scare off the young generation."

Sam stated, "On one hand, I'd love for [the church] to attack the [topics of] homosexuality, race, abortion . . . but that forces the church to take a stand, and I believe the Bible does take a stand, but that forces the church to really put that truth out there and risk scaring off young generations that don't always like to hear the hard truth if it doesn't align with what they believe to be true."

Third, some churches failed to address difficult issues because of a lack of senior leadership. Young adult pastors were equipped and prepared to address the topics that concerned young adults, but sometimes they did not feel they had the backing of senior leadership. One young adult leader said, "When I see humility and vulnerability from senior leaders, I feel comfortable enough to reach out and be like, 'Hey, can I talk to [my group] about some of these things?'" However, he continued, "If I don't see that in somebody, then I'm not going to [open up to the group]."

When senior leadership cultivates a culture of secrecy or hampering questions, it filters down to the young adult groups. In her book *Suffering and the Heart of God*, Diane Langberg explains the devastation a culture of secrecy can leave in its wake: "Many lives have been sacrificed on the altar of secrecy 'for the sake of the church or the mission.'"[2] Many people's faith too. For young adult groups to

---

2. Diane Langberg, *Suffering and the Heart of God: How Trauma Destroys and Christ Restores* (Greensboro, NC: New Growth Press, 2015), Kindle.

have room to express their doubts and questions, wrestling must be modeled from the top down.

Finally, there have not been appropriate venues, forums, or spaces for young adults to air their questions, concerns, or doubts. As mentioned previously, the typical Sunday sermon is one directional. Rarely does a Sunday service involve two-way conversation between the pastor and the congregation, and even if such an opportunity were available, the congregation might not be prepared for such an interaction. Further, larger settings are not conducive to voicing difficult questions or topics because the questioner might fear the judgment of others.

Although a small group setting is probably an easier venue in which to raise concerns or questions, some young adult groups do not provide the opportunity for this to happen. Instead, these groups are constructed like a smaller version of the sermon, with the young adult leaders as the "experts" teaching the "congregation" of young adults. One of our researchers reported, "Within the [young adult] small group, there are weekly conversations on the lesson or the Bible. There wasn't a lot of conversation in regard to *why* they were reading the Bible or what they were getting out of it. The victory was just in listening [to the lesson] and reading."

The researcher continued, "One last observation is of their conversation and body language when transitioning from normal small talk to actual spiritual conversation. Whenever the YA group is discussing movies or sports or something small, there seems to be freedom and enjoyment in the conversation. When the topic shifts to the Bible or God, there is a tension in the air and a lack of desire to enter into the space. It's hard to tell [whether] people feel comfortable or are afraid to say something wrong."

Based on his observations, the researcher believed the leader set the mood and the tone for the group, which hindered their discussion about the thornier issues about the Bible, theology, or societal questions.

READY TO WRESTLE

However, there were also churches that were ready to wrestle.

Some were ready to wrestle with racial injustice. Years ago, when I worked as a research librarian at a small Christian university, my best friend Myrna described to me how she (an African American woman) trained her nephews to walk down a sidewalk. I'm ashamed to admit that it was only after the death (some would call murder) of Elijah McClain that I understood.

Elijah McClain, a young black man who was killed in a Denver suburb, was described as a "soft soul." He loved animals, and he loved making others feel at peace. The evening of August 24, 2019, on the way home after bringing his brother tea, he was stopped by police because he was wearing an open-faced ski mask—not uncommon in the mountain states. The police put him in two carotid holds and gave him a dose of ketamine as a sedative. His last words were, "I'm an introvert. I'm just different that's all. I'm so sorry. I don't have a gun. I don't do that stuff. All I was trying to do was become better. I'll do it. You all are phenomenal. You are beautiful. And I love you. Try to forgive me. I'm sorry."[3]

Several of the churches in our study took part in advocating for Elijah, especially after the death of George Floyd less than a year later. Other churches held panels on the issue of racial injustice. When one researcher asked a group of young adults how they felt about their church hosting a panel on racial injustice, they expressed appreciation and relief. "I do think . . . the church is the ultimate racism breaker because you look in Revelation and it's people from all tribes and tongues. It's not just one tribe and tongue," one young man reflected. "Yet we, when we [seek change in] our neighborhood, ultimately that's

---

3. Stephanie Guerilus, "After Elijah McClain Was Killed by Police, a Petition Signed by More Than 2M Seeks Justice," *Grio*, June 24, 2020, https://the grio.com/2020/06/24 /elijah-mcclain-justice-petition.

what's transforming, not just latching onto a movement [like Black Lives Matter]."

Another person in the group agreed: "I think race relations is absolutely central to the gospel message. And I think we've lost that. I think we've lost sight of Ephesians 2:14–16, where Jesus breaks down the wall and makes the two, one."

Some churches were ready to wrestle with the issue of women in a pastoral role by allowing a woman to deliver the Sunday sermon. This was met with mixed results. One person noted that several people walked into the Sunday service and turned and walked out once they saw a woman was delivering the message. She noted that, in addition to having a woman preach, it would be beneficial to have a discussion around the issue. "I mean the amount of people that can walk into a church and see even a woman onstage and then turn around and walk out . . ." she said. "Where's your heart at? I'd like to see it, talk about that. What're our real priorities? Why does this scare you? And that's what I would want to hear."

Issues such as LGBTQ, sex, and pornography were given less attention in our churches over the course of our study, despite the great number of young adults who wanted to hear about them. Some young adult leaders admitted they wanted to discuss these issues but either lacked the support from senior leadership or the forum to do so.

ADDRESSING ELEPHANTS

So how can we begin to address the elephants in our midst? In their chapter, "From Safe Spaces to Brave Spaces: A New Way to Frame Dialogue around Diversity and Social Justice" in the book *The Art of Effective Facilitation*, Brian Arao and Kristi Clemens argue that the term "safe spaces" has hindered people from having effective dialogue around controversial issues. They write, "We have found with increasing regularity that participants invoke in protest the common ground rules associated with the idea of safe space when the dialogue moves from polite to provocative."[4]

While the concept of safe spaces emerged out of the hope that anxious participants would be reassured they could voice their opinions and concerns during controversial or sensitive discussions, Arao and Clemens suggest that people now conflate "safety" with "comfort," a much lower threshold of tolerance. It is impossible to remove risk from controversial dialogue, and Arao and Clemens argue that "authentic learning about social justice often requires the very qualities of risk, difficulty, and controversy that are defined as incompatible with safety."[5] Rather than continue to use the term *safe spaces*, they suggest constructing "brave spaces" to "emphasize the need for courage rather than the illusion of safety."[6] They suggest the following ground rules for brave spaces:

1. *Engage in controversy with civility.* Rather than simply stating a group must "agree to disagree," which may stymie meaningful dialogue and learning, Arao and Clemens recommend facilitators lay the expectation that differing views will be honored and respected along with a commitment to genuinely understand others' points of view.

2. *Own your own intentions and your impact.* Instead of relying on the old phrase "don't take things personally," individuals should take responsibility for their intentions and their possible impact.

3. *Step up to the challenge by choice.* This ground rule underscores the rights of participants to determine the degree to which they will involve themselves in a controversial or sensitive discussion.

---

4. Brian Arao and Kristi Clemens, "From Safe Spaces to Brave Spaces: A New Way to Frame Dialogue around Diversity and Social Justice," in *The Art of Effective Facilitation* (Sterling, VA: Stylus Publishing, 2013), 135.

5. Ibid., 139.

6. Ibid., 141.

4. *Show respect.* Although many groups begin with a cursory disclaimer to respect the views of all participants, Arao and Clemens believe more time should be spent in the group discussing what respect means. They suggest opening with a question like, "How does someone demonstrate respect to you?" This allows participants greater reflection on what respect means for different people and how they can demonstrate it to others.[7]

Changing the terminology from "safe spaces" to "brave spaces," along with enforcing appropriate ground rules, builds the scaffolding upon which meaningful dialogue can take place around sensitive and controversial subjects. Brave spaces can be woven into the tapestry of ecclesial life in a variety of ways, including forums, interactive panel discussions, workshops, book club discussions, Bible studies, practical theology curriculum, and over dinners with small groups and one-one-one conversations. A community marked by a sincere, thoughtful, earnest engagement with questions and doubts can be demonstrated. But however we do so, we must have the character for it.

Leaders and parents (because parents, too, of course affect the spiritual lives of younger generations) must be willing to "break character" from time to time and admit our own questions and vulnerabilities. "The secret things belong to the LORD our God," heralds Deuteronomy 29:29, "but the things that are revealed belong to us and to our children forever, that we may do all the words of this law." This means there *are* mysteries, things we cannot know, secrets in the universe, maybe fairies in the grass. A sound mind, tradition, and orthodoxy all are important, but the misdirection of the modernists told us there was no limit to our knowledge, that we must know all the answers, that only what is measurable is meaningful. There will be some questions you do not have the answers for.

---

7. Ibid., 143–48.

We have to learn to see the world in full-spectrum color. If social media and unlimited access to almost any culture around the world have taught us anything, it is that we no longer have the luxury of separating issues into neat black and white.

We have learned, again, how to talk to one another. How to listen. How to disagree with civility. How not to cancel or castigate. How to empathize even with our accusers or when it costs us something like time or the extra mile. Sometimes listening means more than a ready answer. It might always mean more.

FACING ELEPHANTS

Haleakalā is the massive shield volcano that covers 75 percent of the island of Maui. The plan was for my dad and daughters to drop me off at one point and pick me up at another. With no cell phone range on or in the volcano and a cold mist steadily sprinkling from the sky, I started to doubt myself. *What am I doing? Can I really finish this in four hours? Is this too ambitious for me?* I looked back to the dropping off point, but my family had already gone. No going back now. There was no choice but to muster the courage to face the elephant before me, the vast moonscape of the volcano.

The icy mist on top of Haleakalā on the island of Maui cleared into a bright day, full sun, as I descended into the volcanic crater. I finished Haleakalā in four hours and fifteen minutes. Not the goal I had in mind at Keonehe'ehe'e trailhead, however well or ill-informed the goal may have been, but not unrespectable either. Some trail guides suggest taking six to nine hours; one ranger told me it took her twelve. Some maps say the trail is twelve miles long; others say it is more like seventeen.

This patchy information, along with moments in the beginning of my journey when visibility seemed near zero, made my goal seem unreachable. There were other moments on the moonscape crater floor when I lost my way, for there was no real trail in that lava sand. It was all . . . "interpretative," as they say in hiking lingo. "Figure it out as you go."

Addressing elephants by creating a listening, empathetic environment in faith communities can seem equally hazardous. How could it not when Christians have seemingly been on the defensive backfoot for several decades? It will be uncomfortable, and in the beginning, visibility may seem to be near zero. We might lose our way in the middle. The trail might be more interpretative than we like. But there are more risks to be taken by not addressing elephants.

We risk further harming the reputation of the church.

We risk the opportunity to model a type of honest, graceful discourse befitting the people of God.

We risk the possibility of speaking meaningfully and masterfully to the surrounding culture.

QUESTIONS FOR INDIVIDUAL AND SMALL GROUP REFLECTION

1. What are the "elephants" your church or faith community has yet to address?
2. Why do you think your faith community avoids these particular issues?
3. Of the four common reasons young adults believe churches do not address controversial issues (avoidance, fear, lack of support from senior leaders, lack of forum), which is most problematic in your faith community? Why?
4. What do you think of the concept of "brave spaces" instead of "safe spaces"?
5. What are the benefits of reframing hard conversations this way? The drawbacks?

6. What other guidelines do you think might be important for faith communities to follow as they seek to build brave spaces?

7. What does it take for you to feel respected? Why?

8. How difficult would it be for you to enter into meaningful dialogue with someone whose opinions diverge from your own?

9. What else does the church risk by not addressing elephants?

FIFTEEN

QUESTION 6

*How Are We Making
a Difference?*

*Our world hangs like a magnificent jewel in
the vastness of space. Every one of us is a part
of that jewel. A facet of that jewel. And in
the perspective of infinity, our differences are
infinitesimal. We are intimately related. May
we never even pretend that we are not.*
—Fred Rogers

R ev. Michael E. Haynes was born in Roxbury, Massachusetts, in 1927 to Barbadian immigrants. When he graduated from the New England School of Theology in 1949, "he thought God was calling him to be a missionary somewhere miles from Boston," but as he continued to serve in Roxbury, he came to understand that, rather than ministering far from Boston, he "was led by God to be a prophet in his home city with a ministry that echoed around the world."[1]

And that he did. Heralded as "the heart and soul and conscience of Boston,"[2] Reverend Haynes pastored Twelfth Baptist Church in his hometown of Roxbury for four decades, from 1964 to 2004. In 1965 he was elected to serve in the Massachusetts House of Representatives, where he and two fellow black legislative colleagues cosponsored a measure inviting his friend, Dr. Martin Luther King Jr., to address a packed joint session of the Legislature. The following day, he joined King in the march from Roxbury to Boston Common to protest racial imbalance in schools and housing. Reverend Haynes served in the House of Representatives from 1965 to 1968 and went on to serve on the state's parole board for sixteen years.

Through his work in the community, investing in the lives of young black men, he influenced hundreds, if not thousands, of lives. But when Dr. James Emery White, the president of Gordon Conwell Theological Seminary, asked him what he did, Reverend Haynes simply said he was a pastor. "Just a little church, in Roxbury. Its ministry is pretty much serving the neighborhood around it," he said. "Those three or four city blocks are what I've given my whole life to. It's been my world."[3]

Three or four city blocks. The life and ministry of Reverend Haynes demonstrates the power of the Holy Spirit to multiply the impact of our ministry efforts. "Then he said to me," proclaimed the prophet Zechariah, "'This is the word of the Lord to Zerubbabel: Not by might, nor by power, but by my Spirit, says the Lord of hosts. Who are you, O great mountain? Before Zerubbabel you shall become

---

1. Advent Christian General Conference, "Rev. Dr. Michael E. Haynes," accessed April 1, 2022, acgc.us/haynes/.

2. Michael Jonas, "The 'Conscience of Boston,'" *Commonwealth*, September 14, 2019, commonwealthmagazine.org/politics/the-conscience-of-boston/.

3. James Emery White, "Being Faithful to a Few City Blocks Can Change the World," Crosswalk.com, January 17, 2007, www.crosswalk.com/faith/spiritual-life/being-faithful-to-a-few-city-blocks-can-change-the-world-1463847.html.

a plain. . . . For whoever has despised the day of small things shall rejoice, and shall see the plumb line in the hand of Zerubbabel (Zech. 4:6–7, 10).'" We should not despise the small things, for it is the work of the Lord to multiply the impact of our efforts.

In today's society, where our level of influence is judged by our number of followers and engagement rates, many of us believe we must expand our reach as far as possible. This is true of individuals as well as churches. In our efforts to extend the reach of our influence, we often miss the opportunities for ministry right in front of us, in our neighborhoods and immediate communities. Yet for young adults, this was one of the most important factors when considering a church: How is the church making a difference in this neighborhood and community?

CHURCHES THAT MAKE A DIFFERENCE

Almost all of the young adults in our study expressed a desire for a church that was investing in their neighborhood. However, according to a study conducted by Springtide research, "When it comes to shared values, half of young people don't think religious insitutions care about the issues that matter to most young people."[4]

In a focus group with several churchgoing young adults, I asked, "How important is it for you that your church be involved in matters of social injustice or social justice? To advocate on behalf of the widows and the orphans? That's biblical social justice, and so how important is it to you for your church to be involved in those things?"

One young woman, Jackie, answered, "I don't think I would ever attend a church that isn't involved in its community and in serving those around it." I asked her why this was important to her. Jackie

---

4. Springtide Research Institute, *The State of Religion and Young People 2021: Navigating Uncertainty* (Winona, MN: St. Mary's Press of Minnesota, 2021), 24.

193

replied, "Because I think that is a call on the church and a call on God's people, and the church that's not doing that is missing part of the purpose of equipping people . . . sending people out is also part of the purpose, to come together to learn more about the Lord and about his heart, and then to go use that to build God's kingdom on earth. I think [if a] church isn't doing that, they're essentially wasting resources or wasting time."

Young adults mentioned several ways they would like to see churches invest their money in their local neighborhood.

First, they suggested investing in immigrants. "I think something that our church could do a lot better at is helping literally the apartments that are directly across the parking lot from us," one young adult, Sofía, said. "Whether that is hosting a movie night where we show *Coco* (because my students love *Coco*, so I'm sure those kids love *Coco*) or hosting a picnic and barbecue." Other suggestions were offering free ESL (English as a second language) classes or assistance with immigrant processing and documentation. In the study conducted by Springtide, 77 percent of young adults stated immigration rights were important to them. When asked if they believed their church communities cared about the issue, only 54 percent said they did.[5]

Second, young adults wanted to provide direct assistance for the neighborhood poor and needy. If churches are not providing help for the local poor and needy, young adults believe those churches are, as Katherine said, "not actually putting our faith where our faith needs to be. Instead we're putting our faith in the American system to take care of the poor and needy." One young man who attended a large black church in a poor community said, "I feel like that is the first thing Jesus did. If we're not doing that, then what are we good for? I like to think of it as: If a church disappeared tomorrow, this church was gone, just out of thin air, would the community notice? Would they realize what they miss? Would they say, 'Oh man, my church is

---

5. Ibid., 34.

gone! How are we going to eat? How are my kids going to be tutored? Those are my friends, those are my people.' The community should know we exist. Feel our impact. That's what Jesus did."

The study by Springtide revealed that 76 percent of young people are concerned about income inequality, with only 53 percent believing their faith communities care about the issue as well.[6]

Third, young adults longed to see their churches address racial injustice. "Social injustice and racism are the opposite of that command that Jesus gave us," Susan said. "So, the obvious thing to do would be to spread the love of Jesus [to racial minorities] any way we can." Another young woman said, "I think as long as the world is here, we're going to have social tensions because social tensions started back in biblical times. If you look at the Ishmaelites versus Abraham and his family, we still have that issue going on. So are social imbalances always going to be there between different nations?" She concluded, "Absolutely. But how do we learn how to mitigate [the imbalances] within our own culture?"

Not surprisingly, although young adults from all of our participating topics mentioned this issue, young adults from all-black or racially diverse churches were more likely to say this was an important issue, if not the most important issue. The Springtide Research group found that racial injustice is important to 81 percent of young people, but only 60 percent of young people believe their churches care about the issue as much as they do.[7]

Fourth, young adults would like their churches to be invested in reproductive rights. Melanie said she appreciated that her church provides support for women who either have had an abortion or were considering an abortion. "Through their actions," she said, "my church is saying, 'Hey, we see the dirt, and we know that it's there. We're not going to ignore it, but here are some resources that can help

---

6. Ibid.
7. Ibid.

you through your struggles.'" Seventy-five percent of young adults who participated in Springtide's research expressed concern about issues related to reproductive rights, but only 54 percent said they believed their churches cared about the issues as well.[8]

The prevailing sentiment among the young adults I spoke with was that the most important thing a church can do is "be out there in the community, but just being present, being out there helping people, being at the forefront of issues and stuff going on in the world." When it comes to the major issues society is struggling with, young adults collectively want to know, "Where is the church? Where's the church represented in this?" Dan mentioned how inspired he was when one pastor said they invited prostitutes to church. "[The unspoken message was] this is not the church for you if you're not going to be welcoming to everybody because the [purpose of] church is not to come and sit in your comfortable bubble," Dan said. "I love how that reaches into our hearts and when a prostitute is welcome to a church the way Jesus welcomed prostitutes to the table that he ate at."

WHY WE TRY TO MAKE A DIFFERENCE

Young adults are not only interested in making a difference in their local communities but also concerned with the motivation behind their and their church's benevolent actions. The young adults I spoke with worried about inappropriate motives and wanted to understand what a healthy motivation could look like.

First, they did not want themselves or their churches to strive for public good just to "out-good" secular people. Young adults wanted to ensure that they and their churches were not just doing good because secular people were. Throughout history, churches were among the first to address societal ills. Today, it has become vogue for

---

8. Ibid.

large companies or even billionaires to at least perpetuate the image of doing good. Young adults want their church to adopt a refreshing approach: doing good for good's sake.

Second, young adults questioned not only their churches' motives but also their own. They worried about performing public good just to feel good about themselves. "It isn't right," Justin said, "for Christians [to do] volunteer work or whatever—reaching out to their community, pulling people, or trying to help people who need help—just to make themselves feel good." He continued, "Of course, you are going to feel good when you help other people out, but that shouldn't be your motivation." They worried that feeling good while doing good invalidated the good they were doing.

Third, young adults did not want to perform altruistic acts just to "become better people" or "be better Christians." They wanted the church to show them how to perform acts of pure altruism, for altruism is an important part of the Christian faith. Throughout the Old and New Testament, Christians are urged to take care of the poor and needy. In Deuteronomy, the Lord explains to the people of Israel, "If among you, one of your brothers should become poor, in any of your towns within your land that the LORD your God is giving you, you shall not harden your heart or shut your hand against your poor brother, but you shall open your hand to him and lend him sufficient for his need, whatever it may be" (15:7–8).

Further, the Lord urges, "Take care lest there be an unworthy thought in your heart . . . You shall give to him freely, and your heart shall not be grudging when you give to him, because for this the LORD your God will bless you in all your work and in all that you undertake. For there will never cease to be poor in the land. Therefore I command you, 'You shall open wide your hand to your brother, to the needy and to the poor, in your land'" (Deut. 15:9–11).

In Jeremiah 22:16, the Lord says, "He judged the cause of the poor and needy; then it was well. Is not this to know me?" In other words, caring for the poor and needy is an essential outcome of knowing God. In his book *Kingdom Conspiracy*, Scot McKnight states that "doing good means disciples are missional in their vocation."[9] McKnight comments, "Our deep calling is to love God and to love others or, in the words of Jesus, to love our neighbor as ourselves."[10] We should strive to be neighborly and to "expand neighboring into 'faithful presence' in all the spaces we occupy."[11] We are not missional or loving in order to become better Christians; being missional and loving are a natural outflow of a heart that is right with God.

THE POLITIC OF JESUS

On the whole, young adults suggested that it was more important for a church to be involved in doing good in their neighborhood than being involved in politics. "I'm not saying they should back off from having hard stances on issues," Tim said, "and I would like the church to educate us on biblical views of political issues, but it is more important to do good in your neighborhood than spouting off on political issues."

The church's role in politics has long been a subject of contention and debate. In 1979, Jerry Falwell Sr. established the right-wing, Republican political organization called the Moral Majority. The Moral Majority campaigned on issues deemed important to the Christian faith, including abortion, divorce, feminism, gay and lesbian rights, and the Equal Rights Amendment. In addition, they endorsed candidates who were most likely to make decisions in alignment with the Christian faith. Although the organization declined and was dismantled in the late 1980s, many young adults still believe that the political mindset of the Moral Majority continues among Christians today.

In *Kingdom Conspiracy*, McKnight says that "kingdom mission

---

9. Scot McKnight, *Kingdom Conspiracy: Returning to the Radical Mission of the Local Church* (Grand Rapids, MI: Brazos Press, 2014), 115.
10. Ibid.
11. Ibid., 116.

as church mission means the church is a kingdom fellowship, or a kingdom politic." [12] Escaping politics is impossible, for "the church is political from the inside out."[13] However, McKnight is quick to add, "To say the church is a politic is not to say the church needs to be more political by becoming more active and aggressive in the political process."[14] Rather, kingdom politics means that "we embody all that the country could be and far more than it is by living out what Jesus calls us to do."[15] A politic of this kind goes far beyond the endorsement of a certain candidate or piece of legislation.

As theologian and ethicist John Howard Yoder commented, "If in society we believe in the rights of employees, then the church should be the first employer to deal with workers fairly. If in the wider society we call for the overcoming of racism or sexism or materialism, then the church should be the place where that possibility first becomes real."[16] This is not to say that society should dictate what the church does (or even what the church calls "good"), but it does urge the church to be a leading force for good.

WAYS TO HELP WELL

Many young adults we spoke with felt that helping neighbors wasn't enough; they wanted to make sure churches helped their neighbors in the right ways. Maria said, "There's always those people who get together bags of clothes and are like, 'Here, you're poor. This is for you because you're poor.'" She continued, "And instead of making people feel welcome and appreciated, it's ostracizing. I know because I've been on the receiving end of a bag of clothes."

---

12. Ibid., 100.
13. Ibid.
14. Ibid., 101.
15. Ibid.
16. John Howard Yoder, The Priestly Kingdom: Social Ethics as Gospel (1984; repr., Notre Dame, Indiana: University of Notre Dame Press, 2001), 93.

These young adults may be on to something. Several studies have found a link between charity and shame. As one study found, "The analysis shows that people receiving charity feel shame, and this shame derives from the judgments of volunteers and the position of recipients as passively receiving what is given."[17] To counteract this dynamic, researchers suggest the following:

1. *Be aware of the dynamic of charity and shame.* For those who serve, it is important to respect and honor the dignity of every individual receiving charity and recognize that the people receiving charity are likely to experience shame.

2. *Consider the manner and attitude in which you distribute charity.* Welcome people with a warm exchange. For example, if serving at a shelter, do not ask, "What do you want?" Instead, invite the person inside into the warmth and enjoin them in a conversation.

3. *Resist judging recipients of charity.* Minister to the needs of others without questioning why they need charity. Many volunteers believe that they themselves have worked for what they have and often cannot understand why one would need charitable outreach. When one is struggling in this manner, it is important to reflect on one's own motivations for participating in outreach. Parsell and Clarke note, "the meaning volunteers ascribed to their own roles as charity providers that influenced their engagement with people and whether charity was likely experienced as shameful."

4. *Listen to their story.* Nothing humanizes a person more than another person taking the time to listen to their story. Listening not only makes a person feel welcomed and heard but also builds understanding and empathy in the heart of the hearer.[18]

---

17. Cameron Parsell and Andrew Clark, "Charity and Shame: Towards Reciprocity," *Social Problems* 69, no. 2 (May 2022): doi.org/10.1093/socpro/spaa057.

18. Ibid.

LIFE OUTSIDE THE CHURCH BUILDING

The church building can be an incarnational presence in the local community. Churches can offer community events that welcome the neighborhood, such as harvest festivals. (My husband and I chose our church because of the harvest festival outreach. Seeing how much of the congregation participated in hosting the neighborhood children was inspiring and told us a lot about how much the church cared for the local community.)

Churches can also invest in their neighborhoods by improving worn-out playgrounds and ensuring the neighborhood is clean, walkable, and vibrant. To reduce urban blight, several ministries in Detroit have popped up to teach residents and youth about urban gardening and have restored abandoned parking lots and playgrounds. When I visited such a ministry, the local youth demonstrated their passion for the garden, and after gardening, we walked through the neighborhood, praying, singing praise songs, and spreading sunflower seeds in an empty lot where a house had been razed. Several youth told me, "Being involved in this ministry has taught me how to bring beauty to my neighborhood, to protect it rather than be destructive."

If your church disappeared, would your neighborhood notice?

QUESTIONS FOR INDIVIDUAL AND SMALL GROUP REFLECTION

1. What are your thoughts about Haynes's commitment to "three or four city blocks"?
2. Do you think it is harder today for Christian leaders to think in those terms? Why or why not?

QUESTIONS AND CHALLENGES

3. What are your thoughts about the issues young adults found important for the church to address? Are there any you would add or take away? Why?

4. Do you agree with Scot McKnight's comment, "Our deep calling is to love God and to love others or, in the words of Jesus, to love our neighbor as ourselves" and that we should strive to be neighborly and to "expand neighboring into 'faithful presence' in all the spaces we occupy"? Why or why not?

5. What is the relationship between charity and shame?

6. What are your ideas for helping others feel less shame about accepting charity?

7. Have you ever felt shame about receiving charity?

8. How do you feel when participating in giving?

9. How can listening alleviate shame?

SIXTEEN

CHALLENGE 6

How Can We Be Good Neighbors?

*No one can say: "Since I'm not called to be
a missionary, I don't have to evangelize my
friends and neighbors." There is no difference, in
spiritual terms, between a missionary witnessing
in his home town and a missionary witnessing in
Katmandu, Nepal. We are all called to go—even
if it is only to the next room, or the next block.*
—Thomas Hale, *On Being a Missionary*

The young pastor, Liam, knew the needs of his neighborhood. His final course at seminary was to develop a plan that would help his church meet the needs of his local community. Liam wanted the young adults to participate. He knew that social work and justice were important to them and also knew that helping others would help grow their faith, not to mention bring them closer together. His community was beset by more problems than his small church could deal with, such as homeless camps, drug use, and high rates of violent crime. So he decided to start small: a neighborhood cleanup on a Saturday, when most people in the community would be home. With any luck, they could start a conversation about their church.

The young adults in Liam's group were enthusiastic about the idea. They wanted to get their hands dirty, meet the people in the houses around the church, and help the neighborhood look better cared for. But when the day came, Liam waited. And waited. Not a single young adult from his group showed up. Several contacted him, bowing out last minute for various reasons, but many never contacted him at all. Liam was disheartened and confused. Young adults had said many times how important it was for churches to impact their local community, but none had followed through and answered the call.

THE MISSIONAL CHURCH

In 1999, I joined a group of women walking around my university, the University of North Texas in Denton, Texas, to raise awareness for the pregnancy center I volunteered at. Beside me, my friend Susan asked, "If you were to go on a mission trip, where would you go?" Newly returned to the faith, I answered, "I think God is calling me here."

"Here?" she replied. "But everyone *here* knows Jesus."

I thought of my former friends and colleagues at work who worked to party, and if they got a degree in the meantime, it was a bonus. No, they did not know Jesus. They came from broken families and broken homes. A friend had been abused by a relative. From the outside, they looked like a group of partiers that did not take life seriously, and that might have been true for some. But most were just trying to survive as best they could with poor, inadequate tools. No one had ever approached them with the gospel in the warm way Jesus approached the Samaritan woman at the well.

Around the same time, Christian theologians, educators, and practitioners were discussing the need to shift missions from "sending out" to different countries to focusing on their immediate communities. Professor Darrell L. Guder noted in 1998, "God's mission is calling and sending us, the church of Jesus Christ, to be a missionary church in our own societies, in the cultures in which we find ourselves. These cultures are no longer Christian; some would argue that they never were."[1] Unfortunately, the terms *missional* and *missional church* can be opaque for some. In an article for *Christianity Today*, J. Todd Billings writes, "Some use *missional* to describe a church that rejects treating the gospel like a commodity for spiritual consumers; others frame it as a strategy for marketing the church and stimulating church growth. Some see the missional church as a refocusing on God's action in the world rather than obsessing over individuals' needs; others see it as an opportunity to 'meet people where they are' and reinvent the church for postmodern culture."[2]

Additionally, the origins of the missional church are marred by its association with the theology and behavior of its earliest adopters, including Rob Bell and Mark Driscoll.

While some of the concerns about the missional movement may be valid, for our purposes, the goal of the missional church movement was to reinforce the theological principle that the church is the incarnational presence of the gospel in a given community. The local church is not nebulous but a concrete presence in the community. In *Missional Church*, Darrell Guder outlines the following five characteristics of the missional church:

---

1. Darrell L. Guder, ed., *Missional Church: A Vision for the Sending of the Church of North America* (Grand Rapids, MI: Eerdmans, 1998), 5.

2. J. Todd Billings, "What Makes a Church Missional?" *Christianity Today*, March 5, 2008, www.christianitytoday.com/ct/2008/march/16.56.html.

1. *A missional church is biblical.* God's people are to be instruments and witnesses of the mission of God.
2. *A missional church is historical.* When shaping our ecclesiology, we must be mindful of those who have preceded us and those who are our contemporaries.
3. *A missional church is contextual.* Every ecclesiology is developed for a specific context.
4. *A missional church is eschatological.* The Holy Spirit is moving God's people to the consummation of all things.
5. *A missional church can be practiced—that is, it can be translated into practice.* The goal of the missional church is to equip the church for its calling.[3]

The principles of the missional church are helpful guidelines for establishing churches that strive to make a difference in their immediate neighborhoods. Most of the churches in our study aspired to begin making a difference right where they were.

THE GAP BETWEEN ASPIRATION AND ACTION

As we learned from the last chapter, young adults desire to be part of churches that make a difference in their local communities. The young adults in our study also expressed a desire to be part of ministry efforts in the local community beyond traditional modes. One young man said, "Food banks [are] this organized, structural thing, and it's been set up and labeled. Yes, you're pouring into the community . . . giving back to the community. But how much of it is just going to your neighbor's house, like, 'Hey, I brought you dinner'? Or just even

---

3. Guder, *Missional Church*, 11–12.

meeting your neighbors because I haven't met any of my neighbors? I see them on the Ring doorbell, but that's about it."

But some pastors offered contrary testimony about the commitment levels of young adults. Most pastors agreed that young adults have a "heart for service" and "want to lead in significant ways" but lack commitment and follow-through.

"Millennials are in love with the idea of public service," one pastor said, "but they have no commitment to follow through." Other pastors echoed the sentiment, with more than one pastor describing young adults as "flaky." As I mentioned at the beginning of the chapter, this became very real for one church, when the young adult pastor planned a community service project with his young adult team, but they "didn't pull it off because none of the young adults showed up the day of."

On July 17, 2018, *Education Week* published the results of a study that reinforces these pastors' perception. "High school and college students are less likely to volunteer or give to charity today than they were 15 years ago," writes Sarah D. Sparks, "even as young adults express the most interest in community engagement in a half-century."[4] In 2015, only 25 percent of young adults volunteered in their communities—down from 28 percent in 2005—thereby ending thirty years of rising volunteerism.[5]

The decline in volunteerism among young adults is part of a larger issue. According to *Bloomberg*, "Fewer Americans are volunteering their time and money on a regular basis. The national volunteer rate has not surpassed 28.8 percent since 2005, and in 2015, it dipped to its lowest, at 24.9 percent."[6] Bloomberg notes that the areas in America

---

4. Sarah D. Sparks, "Volunteerism Declined among Young People," *Education Week*, July 17, 2018, www.edweek.org/leadership/volunteerism-declined-among-young-people/2018/07.

5. Ibid.

6. Linda Poon, "Why Americans Stopped Volunteering," *Bloomberg*, September 11, 2019, https://www.bloomberg.com/news/articles/2019-09-12/america-has-a-post-9-11-volunteerism-slump.

that experienced the largest dip in volunteerism were places with lower home ownership rates and higher economic distress—the very places most in need of volunteers and community service.

This echoes some of the concerns young adults raised about their own volunteerism. While they longed to make a difference in their community, they knew there was a gap between their aspiration and action in the community. They attributed this gap to the following factors:

1. Some young adults were burdened by the demands of college, graduate school, and part-time jobs, leaving little time for them to volunteer.
2. Some who had already graduated from college still worked multiple jobs to afford to raise a family in the expensive Denver metro area.
3. Some mentioned they did not see how volunteering at their church would benefit anyone else, either because they did not agree with the church's service project or because they did not feel as though they had the authority to effect change in their congregations.
4. Some young adults expressed shyness about approaching those already serving on a community project. They wondered if they would be welcomed to join in on what the church was doing.
5. A few young adults expressed doubt about their safety while working in some neighborhoods. Colorado, especially the Denver metro area, has experienced a shocking rise in violent crime in the last few years, with homicides surging to a twenty-five-year high, leaving five people dead every week.[7]

---

7. Elise Schmelzer, "How Bad Is Crime in Colorado? We Examined Thirty-Five Years of Data to Put Today's Trends in Context," *Denver Post*, January 23, 2022, www.denverpost .com/2022/01/23/colorado-crime-rate-homicides-shootings-assaults/.

The gap between aspiration and action can be mitigated with proper preparation and teaching on the importance of being an incarnational presence in the local community.

THE WAY CHURCHES SERVED

Throughout the duration of the project, several churches made strong efforts to influence their local communities. First, churches gathered food for the poor. At least three churches operated large-scale food banks where people in the community could get free or deeply discounted food and supplies (e.g., cleaning supplies and diapers). Other churches joined with outside ministries, and hundreds in the congregation would put food boxes together for thousands of people.

Second, churches provided clothing for disadvantaged people through clothing drives and donating "an item of the month."

Third, churches offered camps for foster children and tutoring for lower-income children.

Fourth, churches invested in the beautification of their neighborhoods by restoring parks and playgrounds and having regular cleanup drives.

Fifth, churches provided legal aid, accounting advice, and ESL training, and they sought to help immigrants seek asylum.

Sixth, churches went door to door in their immediate neighborhoods, letting the neighbors know they were there, and if they needed anything, to simply reach out. Many elderly neighbors took them up on this offer, stating there were things around the house they were no longer able to do. The church helped them around their houses and cleaned their lawns.

Seventh, churches participated in protests for certain causes, including the deaths (murders) of George Floyd and Elijah McClain.

So, despite the impression young adults had that their churches were not doing anything in their local communities, churches did a great deal of good in their neighborhoods.

THE WAY TO BE GOOD NEIGHBORS

To fight the downward trend in volunteerism and to close the gap between young adults' aspirations and their perception of the church's good acts, there are six things churches can do:

1. *Teach young adults about leadership and service.* One pastor said, "I know that young adults often say they want to serve and then don't, but we have to show we believe in them." Regular teaching on leadership and service, grounded in the Scriptures, is critical to helping students understand how to serve their community. Building their knowledge on a theological foundation provides a firmer grasp on why leadership and service are important to the heart of God.

2. *Teach young adults the connection between service and psychological well-being.* In Acts 20:35, the apostle Paul quotes Jesus, "In all things I have shown you that by working hard in this way we must help the weak and remember the words of the Lord Jesus, how he himself said, 'It is more blessed to give than to receive.'" Thousands of studies have confirmed this maxim and demonstrate a proven correlation between serving others and improved mood, reduced stress, improved self-esteem, and even a longer life.

3. *Clearly promote opportunities to serve.* While some young adults mentioned their churches required some volunteerism in order to become a member, other churches simply need to make young adults aware of service opportunities. Since many young adults attend only the young adult group, it is important to advertise these opportunities on message boards, social

media profiles, and through the young adult leaders. Young adults love to serve as groups, so providing opportunities for them to do so can help them better understand the importance of volunteerism. Let people know about the time commitment expected for each project.

4. *Evaluate the needs of your immediate community.* While food banks are important, many young adults are interested in learning how to serve people on a one-on-one basis. As one young man said, "I'd like to learn how to be more comfortable approaching my neighbor and bringing them dinner." This, of course, requires an intimate knowledge of the needs of your neighborhood.

5. *Evaluate the needs of nearby communities.* Rather than thinking with a competitive mindset about nearby churches, think more collaboratively about how neighboring churches can come together to benefit the community.

THE WAY IN THE NEIGHBORHOOD

At the beginning of the Kaleo Project, Eastside Church was just beginning. When seeking to plant a church, a group of leaders from Mexico and several South American countries looked at the poorest neighborhoods in the Denver metro area. In one neighborhood, they saw an abandoned Methodist church. When they contacted the Methodist headquarters, they were offered a one-hundred-year rental contract rather than the opportunity to purchase the church and the land. Though the church was in a serious state of disrepair, they were not deterred. Before the church even opened, they went from door to door introducing themselves. At first, people were suspicious of their motivations, but soon people got to know them and began to trust them.

The pastors set about restoring the church, and they were delighted to be joined by several neighbors. Today, Eastside Church holds weekly free breakfasts and packs lunches almost daily for children who can grab a sack lunch on their way to the bus stop. When you ask the neighbors, they say the church has been an enormous blessing both to their community and to them personally. They say they feel valued, seen, and known.

QUESTIONS FOR INDIVIDUAL AND SMALL GROUP REFLECTION

1. Do you think it is the responsibility of wealthier churches to be aware of the needs of their poorer neighbors? Why or why not?
2. Should churches adopt a missional mindset? Why or why not?
3. What would a missional mindset look like at your church?
4. Do you know about the service opportunities at your church? Why or why not?
5. Are you able to work with your church to serve your local community on a regular basis? Why or why not?
6. What would you need to change in order to increase your volunteerism?
7. What do you think about the gap between the importance young adults put on volunteerism and their actual participation in volunteerism?
8. Why do you think this gap exists?
9. What are some ways that your church can help young adults increase their volunteerism?

CONCLUSION

The Unspoken Question

[Hope] is a firm advance towards a masked future.
—Brian McGaffigan, "Hope in Time of Abandonment"

This book is a book of questions. Questions young adults have about the church and questions pastors have about how to answer well. These questions are rooted in research. They are what we heard and witnessed from the young adults and pastors with whom we worked.

But there is another question I think young adults and pastors alike are asking: What good can *I* do? The question is unspoken, perhaps buried under an avalanche of doubts or maybe even excuses.

What good can I do in a world that can be shut down by a pandemic? A plague that cost more than six million people their lives and cost many others their livelihoods?

What good can I do in a world teeming with unrest between countries? When China or Russia rattles their swords, when Ukrainians hide from mortar attacks in subways or need medicine for the radiation from Chernobyl?

What good can I do about our divided nation, about the opioid crisis, homelessness, or human trafficking?

I have asked these questions at various periods of my life. When I was young, I knew the world held trouble even before I saw it with my own eyes through the internet. But I held on to the hope that God could use me to make the world a better place. What good could I do when I was just a child? What good could I do when I was just a college student? What good could I do when I was just a poet, a stay-at-home mom of two daughters? What good can I do when my schedule is loaded to the brim?

The truth is there are always opportunities to do good. As a child, I could remind my grandparents in their grief that God was still good. As a college student, I could comfort my friends, bringing them hot, homemade meals when they were feeling homesick. As a poet and a mom, I could raise daughters who would, in time, do good of their own. When my schedule is loaded to the brim, I can remember to be kind. To go the extra mile. I can surprise people with goodness.

It is easy to believe that young adults are a hopeless case. The onslaught of quantative data seems to tell us the church has lost them. But Jesus has not lost them. He knows them, loves them, and wants them to be in relationship with him. And he can use us, with the gifts he has bestowed upon us, to find them, to help them—not to give up on them. To reach them and teach them about the good they can do.

It is easy to believe the church in America is a hopeless case. The church has lost its cultural and political authority. It is crippled by terrible scandals. More churches are closing their doors than opening. Pastors and other Christian leaders may feel like they are going down with the unsinkable ship. But Jesus has not lost his authority or power. Jesus is not crippled by scandal. Jesus has not lost hope for his bride, the church.

However grim our world or circumstances may seem, the God of hope is still the God of hope, and no person or church is a hopeless case.